QUESTIONS & ANSWERS:
The First Amendment

QUESTIONS & ANSWERS:
The First Amendment

Second Edition

RUSSELL L. WEAVER
Professor of Law & Distinguished University Scholar
University of Louisville
Louis D. Brandeis School of Law

WILLIAM D. ARAIZA
Professor of Law
Brooklyn Law School

ISBN: 978-1-4224-7709-0

NOTE TO USERS

To ensure that you are using the latest materials available in this area, please be sure to periodically check the LexisNexis Law School web site for downloadable updates and supplements at www.lexisnexis.com/lawschool.

Editorial Offices
121 Chanlon Rd., New Providence, NJ 07974 (908) 464-6800
201 Mission St., San Francisco, CA 94105-1831 (415) 908-3200
www.lexisnexis.com

MATTHEW⬥BENDER

DEDICATIONS

To Ben and Kate, with love, RLW

To Stephen, WDA

ABOUT THE AUTHORS

RUSSELL L. WEAVER is Professor of Law and Distinguished University Scholar at the University of Louisville's Louis D. Brandeis School of Law. During his twenty-three years at the University of Louisville, he has visited at a number of U.S. law schools, including the South Texas College of Law, where he held the Judge Spurgeon Bell Distinguished Professorship, and the University of Memphis' Cecil C. Humphreys School of Law where he held the Herbert Herff Chair of Excellence. In addition, he regularly visits at a number of foreign schools, including the University of Montpellier in France, and the Johannes Guttenburg University in Germany. He has also visited at law schools in England, Canada, Japan and Australia.

Professor Weaver has taught the First Amendment, and other constitutional law courses, for more than twenty years. In addition, he has authored or co-authored dozens of books and articles including numerous First Amendment and Constitutional Law texts. *See* D. LIVELY, P. HADDON, D. ROBERTS, R. WEAVER & W. ARAIZA, CONSTITUTIONAL LAW: CASES, HISTORY AND DIALOGUES (2d ed., Lexis Nexis, 1999); D. LIVELY, D. ROBERTS & R. WEAVER, THE FIRST AMENDMENT ANTHOLOGY (Lexis Nexis 1996); R. WEAVER & A. HELLMAN, THE FIRST AMENDMENT: CASES, MATERIALS AND PROBLEMS (Lexis Nexis 2002); R. WEAVER & D. LIVELY, UNDERSTANDING THE FIRST AMENDMENT (2004).

WILLIAM D. ARAIZA is Professor of Law at Brooklyn Law School. Professor Araiza has been a professor and associate dean at Loyola Law School Los Angeles, an adjunct professor at UCLA Law School, and a visiting professor at The University of California, Hastings College of Law, Washington and Lee University School of Law, Lewis & Clark Law School, and the University of Western Ontario.

Professor Araiza is the author of numerous articles on constitutional and administrative law, and has co-authored CONSTITUTIONAL LAW: CASES, HISTORY AND DIALOGUES (3rd ed., Lexis Nexis 2006) (with P. Haddon, D. Roberts and M. I. Medina) and FIRST AMENDMENT LAW: FREEDOM OF EXPRESSION AND FREEDOM OF RELIGION (2nd ed. Lexis Nexis 2010) (with A. Hellman and T. Baker).

PREFACE

The First Amendment to the United States Constitution contains some of the most important provisions in the Constitution. Perhaps the most important provision is its sweeping language protecting freedom of speech and of the press. But the First Amendment also contains the religion clauses, which prevent government from "establishing" a religion and guarantee all citizens the right to freely exercise their religion.

Although the First Amendment applies by its term only to Congress (it states that "Congress shall make no law. . . ."), it has been broadly interpreted to apply to all three branches of the federal government. In addition, it has been incorporated into the Fourteenth Amendment to the United States Constitution and applied to the states.

The purpose of this book is to test your understanding of First Amendment law, and to assist you in preparing for a First Amendment or Constitutional Law examination. This book is not intended to provide a comprehensive explanation of First Amendment concepts, but as a supplement to class materials.

This book examines the major First Amendment subjects and concludes with a comprehensive Final Exam. In the speech section of the book, we focus on such topics as hate speech, advocacy of illegal action, commercial speech, campaign finance, defamation, obscenity, public forum doctrine, and symbolic speech. In the religion section, we focus on free exercise, as well as on government support for religion, school prayer, creche displays, evolution, the Ten Commandments, and a host of other issues.

As you utilize these Questions, remember that there may not be a single correct answer, but there might be a "best answer." In other words, you might be asked to make informed judgments based on your knowledge of First Amendment law and your wisdom.

Professor Russell L. Weaver
Louisville, KY
Professor William D. Araiza
Brooklyn, NY
May, 2010

TABLE OF CONTENTS

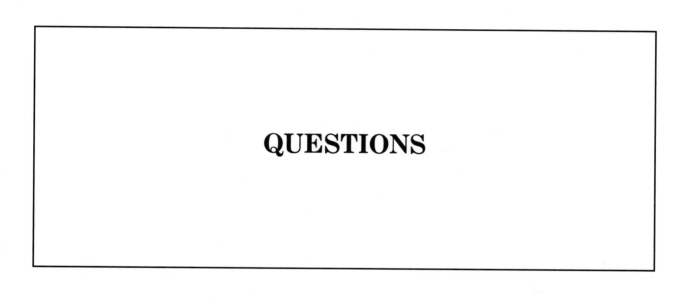

QUESTIONS

PART I
FREEDOM OF SPEECH

QUESTIONS

1.1.   The First Amendment protects freedom of speech and of the press in broad and unqualified terms. Under current United States Supreme Court interpretations, this language is construed to mean that:

(A)   The First Amendment is "absolute" so that the freedoms of speech and press are "completely out of the area of any congressional control."

(B)   First Amendment rights are not "absolute."

(C)   First Amendment rights can be abridged only when a compelling governmental interest exists.

(D)   First Amendment rights can be abridged whenever a "substantial governmental interest" exists.

1.2.   In evaluating the drafters' intent regarding the meaning of the First Amendment, it is safe to say that:

(A)   Evidence regarding the Framers' intent is murky, at best, because the need for speech protections was so widely held that there was no perceived need to articulate the justifications for protecting speech.

(B)   Evidence regarding the Framers' intent is relatively detailed and provides much guidance to those seeking to apply the First Amendment today.

(C)   The records of the Constitutional Convention provide much evidence regarding intent.

(D)   No records were kept at the Constitutional Convention.

1.3.   In evaluating the reasons why the American people might have been motivated to demand special protections for speech, which of the following statements is *incorrect*:

(A)   The people were aware that speech had been repressed in the colonies by means of the crime of seditious libel.

(B)   The people were aware that speech had been repressed in England and the colonies by virtue of licensing restrictions.

(C)   There was a widespread popular perception that freedom of speech was entitled to special protections.

(D)   The Framers hoped to continue the centuries-old English tradition against libel laws and "taxes on knowledge."

1.4.   In English common law, which of the following elements or ideas was **not** true regarding the crime of seditious libel?

(A)   The law provided criminal punishment for criticism of governmental officials.

(B)   The law provided criminal punishment only for false criticisms of government (true criticisms were permitted).

(C)   At one time, the law punished not only those who criticized governmental officials but also those who criticized the clergy.

(D)   Among the sanctions that could be imposed on those who committed seditious libel was the punishment of imprisonment.

1.5.   Numerous justifications have been offered for the special status accorded to speech under the First Amendment. Which of the following is not one of the justifications:

(A)   The "marketplace of ideas."

(B)   That free speech is a necessary aspect of democratic government.

(C)   Self-fulfillment.

(D)   Mass ranking theory.

1.6.   Which additional theories have been advanced in support of the special status accorded to speech under the First Amendment: REDO

(A)   The "anything goes" theory (*i.e.*, the theory that any speech on any topic is necessarily valuable enough to be protected, regardless of the consequences).

(B)   The "safety valve" theory (*i.e.*, the theory that speech is valuable as a way of letting people express themselves in ways short of violence or lawlessness).

(C)   The "as long as it does not harm" theory (*i.e.*, the theory that speech should be protected as long as it does not directly harm anyone).

(D)   The "no undue intrusion" theory (*i.e.*, the theory that speech should be allowed as there is no undue intrusion on the rights of others..

1.7.   Please write a short answer explaining the "safety valve" theory of free speech.

ANSWER:

1.8. Under the marketplace of ideas justification for protecting freedom of expression, which of the following statements is true?

(A) The theory presumes that ideas have economic value, and that they are bartered and sold like other commodities.

(B) The theory assumes that legislation is bought and sold by means of deals and compromises.

(C) The theory assumes that, once ideas are allowed to compete against each other, the government will eventually issue a declaration recognizing which idea has prevailed in the marketplace.

(D) While the marketplace theory assumes that ideas will compete against each other, it does not provide a mechanism for declaring which ideas have prevailed (other than the fact that the citizenry can express their preferences through the ballot box).

1.9. Some have construed the "marketplace of ideas" theory as suggesting that free speech necessarily leads to a "competition of ideas" in the "marketplace of ideas," and that this competition necessarily leads to the triumph of "truth" or the best ideas. Please write a short answer explaining whether this view is accurate and whether the "marketplace of ideas" theory is sustainable without it.

ANSWER:

1.10. Which of the following statements is not a correct statement regarding the democratic process theory?

(A) In a democracy, truth flows not from the government to the people, but from the people to the government.

(B) In a democracy, the citizens must have the freedom to debate ideas and issues as an essential part of the democratic process and the right to vote.

(C) The democratic process theory only protects speech at or near the time of elections.

(D) Without freedom of speech, there is no democracy.

1.11. Explain why free speech is necessary to the democratic process.
ANSWER:

2.1.   Tom, a radical animal rights activist, speaks at a rally in front of the corporate headquarters of Smith and Mann, a major cosmetics firm that uses animals in testing cosmetics. Growing progressively louder and more impassioned, Tom's speech reaches a climax when he says, "We've had enough of the cosmetic companies' promises to mend their ways. The torture must end! It must end now!" The crowd starts to chant, "It must end now, it must end now." After five minutes of chanting the crowd breaks through the door of the headquarters building and causes serious damage. Tom is arrested for inciting a riot. Does the First Amendment provide Tom with a defense?

(A)   YES, because Tom's speech concerns matters of political and social policy at the core of the First Amendment.

(B)   NO, because speakers are held to the consequences of their actions.

(C)   YES, because Tom will be held not to have intended an immediate riot.

(D)   YES, because the facts do not say that he actually participated in the riot.

2.2.   Which of the following statements best describes the current state of the law regarding speech that incites unlawful action?

(A)   Speakers are held to the desired consequences of their action; thus, any speech that suggests unlawful conduct can be prohibited.

(B)   Any speech that actually causes unlawful action can be punished as incitement.

(C)   Any speech that intends to cause immediate unlawful action and that has a likelihood of actually inciting it can be punished as incitement.

(D)   Speech cannot be punished unless the speaker participates in the ensuing unlawful conduct.

2.3.   Which of the following people would be most likely to be validly convicted for inciting a riot?

(A)   A speaker at a rally who gives an impassioned but abstract speech that rouses the crowd to violence.

    (B)   A speaker who rants at passersby on a sidewalk near police headquarters, urging people to burn the headquarters down, but who is ignored.

    (C)   A speaker who delivers an impassioned address at a tense rally, making several calls for immediate action against a nearby target, which the crowd then attacks.

    (D)   A speaker at a rally who makes explicit calls for violence, who finishes his speech and then sits down; several hours later the crowd riots.

2.4.   A local Klu Klux Klan (KKK) group gets together once a month to sing songs, make racist statements (calling for "revenge" against various groups), and burn a large cross. Explain whether the KKK participants in the rally can be successfully prosecuted for advocating illegal action . If you need further information to come to a firm conclusion, explain what information you need and why you need it.

ANSWER:

3.1.   In its decision in *Chaplinsky v. New Hampshire*, 315 U.S. 568 (1942), the Supreme Court held that certain categories of speech are entitled to no protection under the First Amendment to the United States Constitution. In *Chaplinsky*, which of the following statements did the Court **not** make regarding this categorical approach to speech?

(A)   The excluded categories of speech have no speech value whatsoever.

(B)   The excluded categories of speech have such "slight value" towards the ascertainment of truth that they are not constitutionally protected.

(C)   Among the excluded categories of speech are the lewd and the obscene, and the profane.

(D)   Among the excluded categories of speech are libelous and insulting speech, as well as fighting words.

3.2.   *Chaplinsky* was a "fighting words" decision. In other words, the Court held that fighting words are not protected under the First Amendment to the United States Constitution. Which of the following justifications did the Court **not** offer regarding the fighting words exception?

(A)   Fighting words are words that are likely to provoke an immediate, violent response.

(B)   Fighting words are not constitutionally protected because they are insulting, as well as because they offend basic concepts of human dignity.

(C)   Fighting words are not compatible with the marketplace of ideas theory because they are likely to provoke a response before reasoned discourse can occur.

(D)   Fighting words have only slight value in the marketplace of ideas.

3.3.   There are certain categories of speech that are unprotected under the First Amendment, such as so-called "fighting words." In the range of protected/unprotected speech, it is safe to say that "offensive speech":

(A)   Never receives special protection under the First Amendment because "offensive" speech has no value.

(B)   Always receives special protection

(C)   Sometimes receives special protection.

(D)   Is not protected because of its offensive nature.

3.4.   Which of the following was not part of the holding in *Cohen v. California*, 403 U.S. 15 (1971):

(A)   The state lacked the power to punish Cohen for the content of his message.

(B)   A prohibition on "offensive speech" failed to put Cohen on notice that his conduct might be prohibited in a courthouse.

(C)   Context matters when considering claims that offensive speech is constitutionally protected.

(D)   Vulgar speech is unprotected.

3.5.   Please write a short answer discussing whether words should only be protected because of their rational or persuasive value rather than their emotive value.

ANSWER:

3.6.   *FCC v. Pacifica Foundation*, 438 U.S. 726 (1978), involved George Carlin's monologue entitled "Filthy Words." In this monologue, he repeatedly uses the seven filthy words, which he describes as the words banned from the airwaves by the FCC. When the Pacific Foundation aired the monologue as part of a program on contemporary attitudes towards speech, and the Federal Communications Commission issued a declaratory order indicating that the Foundation could be punished for airing the program, the United States Supreme Court held that:

(A)   Under the precedent established in *Cohen v. California*, 403 U.S. 15 (1971), the Carlin monologue was absolutely protected under the First Amendment.

(B)   Because broadcasting is a uniquely pervasive medium, and because the Carlin monologue was "patently offensive," though not necessarily obscene, it is subject to regulation by channeling it to times of the day when children most likely would not be exposed to it.

(C)   The Federal Communications Commission did not have the statutory power to regulate offensive speech being aired over broadcast media.

(D)   The Carlin monologue did not violate any FCC rule.

3.7.   *National Endowment for the Arts v. Finley*, 524 U.S. 569 (1998), involved a congressional requirement that the National Endowment for the Arts (NEA) consider "general standards of decency and respect for the diverse beliefs and values of the American public" in making awards. In that case, the Court held that:

(A) The NEA statute should be upheld because it simply required the NEA to take "general standards of decency and respect for the diverse beliefs and values of the American public" into account in making grants.

(B) Under *Cohen v. California*, 403 U.S. 15 (1971), Congress did not have the power to regulate so-called offensive speech.

(C) Congress cannot mandate "general standards of decency."

(D) Congress has broad power to proscribe indecent speech.

3.8. *Erznoznik v. City of Jacksonville*, 422 U.S. 205 (1975), involved a facial challenge to a Jacksonville, Florida, ordinance that prohibited the showing of films containing nudity by a drive-in movie theater when its screen is visible from a public street or place. Although the films were not "obscene" under the *Miller v. California* standard, the state argued that it could protect its citizens against unwilling exposure to materials that may be offensive. In *Erznoznik*:

(A) The Court held that "offensive material" could be zoned to places where it would not be viewed by unwilling citizens, particularly children.

(B) Relying on its prior holding in *Cohen v. California*, 403 U.S. 15 (1971), the Court held that the burden normally falls upon the viewer to "avoid further bombardment of [his] sensibilities simply by averting [his] eyes."

(C) The Court did not rely on *Cohen* because the medium involved in *Erznoznik* (a drive-in movie theater) is so dramatically different than the broadcast media involved in *Cohen*.

(D) The Court held that municipalities have broad power to regulate the content of drive-in movie theaters.

3.9. The American Socialist Nazi Party (American Nazis) wishes to hold a parade (march) in Skokie, Illinois, even though several thousand survivors of the Nazi holocaust live in that city. Among the American Nazis' more controversial and generally unacceptable beliefs are that black persons are biologically inferior to white persons, and should be expatriated to Africa as soon as possible, and that American Jews have "inordinate . . . political and financial power" in the world and are "in the forefront of the international Communist revolution." American Nazi members wear a uniform reminiscent of those worn by members of the German Nazi Party during the Third Reich, and display a swastika on a red, white, and black Nazi flag. The City of Skokie has refused to issue a parade permit on the basis that the march would be "offensive" and might invoke religious hatred. Write a short answer suggesting whether the permit can be denied based on the "offensive" nature of the speech.

ANSWER:

3.10. Sid Scupper is a white supremacist who assaults an African-American who has moved into Sid's neighborhood. Sid is charged, tried, and convicted of assault, and a jury also finds that the assault was racially-motivated. The jury's finding of racial motivation triggers a longer sentence, under a statute that increases sentences when violent crimes are racially motivated. Sid contests the lengthier sentence, on the ground that it penalizes his thoughts and thus violates the First Amendment. How should the court rule on Sid's claim?

(A) It should REJECT the claim; the statute penalizes conduct, not thought, and thus does not violate the First Amendment.

(B) It should ACCEPT the claim, as the statute penalizes thought.

(C) It should ACCEPT the claim, not because the statute penalizes thought, but because it does so in a content-based manner, i.e., by imposing burdens on racial motivation that it does not burden on other types of motivation.

(D) It should REJECT the claim, because its penalization of thought is viewpoint neutral.

3.11. Assume that, instead of assaulting his neighbor, Sid burns a cross on the neighbor's lawn, leading the district attorney to charge him with violation of a city ordinance that makes it a misdemeanor "to instill fear of assault on the basis of the victim's race, gender, religion or sexual orientation." Sid again defends by arguing that his conduct is protected by the First Amendment. How should the court rule on Sid's defense?

(A) Sid wins because the ordinance is a content-based restriction on expression, and thus will be subject to strict scrutiny, which it probably cannot survive.

(B) Sid loses because speech instilling fear in another is the equivalent of fighting words, which are constitutionally unprotected.

(C) Sid loses because even though the words are fighting words (which enjoy only minimal constitutional protection), an ordinance like this would survive since it is clearly aimed at eliminating racial and other tensions in the city.

(D) Sid wins because fighting words, as speech that is highly expressive, is fully protected by the First Amendment.

3.12. Lee Lightningrod is an iconoclastic holder of unconventional opinions. One day he marches (legally, under a permit) with his supporters to City Hall, where he begins a nasty tirade against the mayor and city council, both of whom are extremely popular. As Lee's speech gets more and more outrageous, with claims of sexual misconduct and gross racial discrimination, onlookers begin to jeer, although at no point was there an indication that violence was on the verge of breaking out, and the police had adequate resources on hand to keep the situation calm at least for the time being. After making an initial attempt to restrain the increasingly hostile crowd, the police captain in charge mounts the makeshift stage where Lee is speaking and demands that he stop speaking or face arrest for inciting a riot. When Lee refuses, he is arrested. Please write a short answer discussing whether Lee can be validly convicted?

ANSWER:

3.13. The State of South Carolina enacts a law prohibiting cross-burning. Tom and David, neighbors, have a serious argument which leads Tom to burn a cross on David's lawn. He is charged with violating the statute and defends based on the First Amendment. How should the court rule on Tom's defense?

(A) Tom wins, because cross-burning is an act that often has racial overtones, and therefore an anti-cross burning statute is unconstitutional as a content-based restriction on fighting words.

(B) Tom loses, because the cross-burning statute does not single out expression of racial views, but simply bans all cross burning.

(C) Tom loses, because cross burning is conduct rather than speech and thus has no First Amendment protection.

(D) Tom wins unless the State can show that the cross-burning attempted to convey a message of intimidation based on race.

3.14. Bob Baker, a pamphleteer for a religious group called The Christian Missionaries, is handing out pamphlets on the topic on a street corner in Watertown. After a police officer attempts to force Baker to move on and to stop his activities, Baker unleashes a torrent of verbal abuse against the officer. Baker never threatens the officer with physical violence, but otherwise he calls him every bad name he can think of. The officer arrests Baker for disturbing the peace. Should the conviction stand?

(A) NO: all Baker ever did was use abusive language, there was never a threat of physical violence, and thus Baker's speech was protected.

(B) YES: the Supreme Court has held that some words naturally lead a reasonable listener to fight rather than to respond with counterspeech, and such abusive speech can constitutionally be prohibited.

(C) YES: the Supreme Court has held that a city has an interest in public decorum and peace such that unpleasant language can be banned, even if that language is not seriously abusive to any particular individual.

(D)   NO: Baker had a right to proselytize on city streets, and any attempt to arrest him for exercising that right would be invalid.

3.15.   Paul Politico leads a group of marchers in a political parade which starts out peacefully. When the parade reaches its end, Paul gives a speech. A group of counter-demonstrators gathers and the police grow nervous that violence may ensue, especially as the speech becomes more and more impassioned. At a certain point the police ask Paul to stop speaking, to prevent the possibility of a riot. Paul refuses and the police arrest him for inciting a riot. Would a court affirm the conviction?

(A)   Probably, since any time the police suspect that violence may ensue from a speech, they may demand that the speaker stop speaking.

(B)   Probably not, because the First Amendment requires that the police try to control the hostile crowd before arresting the speaker.

(C)   Probably not, because a hostile crowd can never justify the police in arresting a speaker.

(D)   Probably, as long as the police advised Paul that his speech was arousing hostility in the crowd, and gave him a chance to tone down his words.

3.16.   Prior to the United States Supreme Court's holding in *New York Times Co. v. Sullivan*, 376 U.S. 254 (1964), the Court:

(A)   Treated defamatory speech as protected speech, but gave it less protection than political speech.

(B)   Held that defamatory speech fell into a category of speech that was not protected under the First Amendment.

(C)   Held that defamatory speech was entitled to full protection under the First Amendment.

(D)   Held that defamatory speech should be treated exactly like political speech.

3.17.   Prior to the holding in *New York Times Co. v. Sullivan*, 376 U.S. 254 (1964), which of the following statements was true:

(A)   States had broad authority to define the tort of defamation.

(B)   States had no authority to define the tort of defamation.

(C)   States had limited authority to define the tort of defamation provided that they acted consistently with existing (and extensive) federal defamation laws.

(D)   States could define the tort of defamation only to the extent that Congress allowed them to do so.

3.18.   In *New York Times Co. v. Sullivan*, 376 U.S. 254 (1964), the United States Supreme Court did not articulate which of the following propositions:

(A)   Alabama's defamation rules, premised as they were on the common law, were unconstitutional.

(B)   Erroneous statement is inevitable in free debate, and [it] must be protected if the freedoms of expression are to have the "breathing space" that they "need [to] survive."

(C)   Injury to official reputation affords no more warrant for repressing speech that would otherwise be free than does factual error.

(D)   Alabama had broad authority to define the tort of defamation.

3.19.   Please explain the "actual malice" standard articulated in *New York Times Co. v. Sullivan*, 376 U.S. 254 (1964).

ANSWER:

3.20.   In *New York Times Co. v. Sullivan*, 376 U.S. 254 (1964), the United States Supreme Court articulated which of the following propositions:

(A)   In order to provide greater protection for free speech, judges rather than juries should hear defamation cases.

(B)   In order to provide greater protection for free speech, public officials should be barred from bringing defamation suits.

(C)   In a defamation case by a public official, the plaintiff bears the burden of proving actual malice.

(D)   In a defamation case by a public official, defendant has the burden of proving that he acted without actual malice.

3.21   Please describe how the historical crime of seditious libel played into the Court's analysis in in *New York Times Co. v. Sullivan*, 376 U.S. 254 (1964).

ANSWER:

3.22.   In *New York Times Co. v. Sullivan*, 376 U.S. 254 (1964), the Court held that:

(A)   In lieu of the actual malice defense, a state may impose a defense of truth and thereby comply with constitutional requirements.

(B)   If the actual malice standard is satisfied, a state may "presume" damages in a defamation case.

(C)   In a defamation case, an appellate court must independently examine the entire record in deciding whether to uphold a defamation award, and must find that it is supported by "convincing clarity."

(D)   In a defamation case, private plaintiffs should be held to a different burden of proof than public officials.

3.23.   In *Curtis Publishing Co. v. Butts*, 388 U.S. 130 (1967), the United States Supreme Court:

(A)   Abandoned the "actual malice" standard as unworkable.

(B)   Extended the "actual malice" standard to public figures.

(C)   Modified the "actual malice" standard to permit recovery based on simple negligence in some instances.

(D)   Adopted a "gross negligence" standard.

3.24.   Which of the following statements is inconsistent with the holding in *Curtis Publishing Co. v. Butts*, 388 U.S. 130 (1967):

(A)   The public interest in the material relating to public figures is as great as material relating to public officials.

(B)   As a public figure, Butts (the plaintiff) had sufficient access to the media to allow him to counter any false statements.

(C)   Libel actions by public figures cannot be left to the dictates of state law without any constitutional protections.

(D)   The law has always treated public figures similarly to public officials.

3.25.   In *Gertz v. Robert Welch, Inc.*, 418 U.S. 323 (1974), the Court held that:

(A)   *Curtis Publishing* should be overruled and lesser liability standards should be applied to public figures.

(B)   Attorneys who have some relationship to high profile criminal cases should also be subjected to the actual malice standard.

(C)   Private individuals should be distinguished from public officials and public figures, and subjected to lesser liability standards.

(D)   Private individuals should be treated similarly to public figures.

3.26. In *Gertz v. Robert Welch, Inc.*, 418 U.S. 323 (1974), the Court did ***not*** offer which of the following justifications for applying lesser liability standards to private individuals:

(A) The states have a legitimate interest in providing compensation to private individuals who have been defamed.

(B) The actual malice standard exacts a high price from plaintiffs (making it more difficult for them to recover for injury to reputation) and this price might not be appropriate as applied to private individuals.

(C) Public officials and public figures have greater access to the media than private individuals, and therefore have the ability to exercise self-help by responding to defamation allegations.

(D) Private individuals deserve no constitutional protection.

3.27 In *Gertz v. Robert Welch, Inc.*, 418 U.S. 323 (1974), the Court held that which of the following liability standards could be applied by states to defamation actions by private individuals:

(A) Strict liability.

(B) There can be no recovery of presumed or punitive damages, at least when liability is not based on a showing of knowledge of falsity or reckless disregard for the truth.

(C) Gross negligence.

(D) Liability without fault.

3.28. Discuss whether punitive damages are appropriate in defamation actions by private individuals.

ANSWER:

3.29. In *Dun & Bradstreet, Inc. v. Greenmoss Builders, Inc.*, 472 U.S. 749 (1985), in a plurality opinion, the Court held that the states enjoy more latitude to establish liability standards in defamation cases involving private plaintiffs and matters of purely private concern, compared to cases involving public figures and matters of public concern. Which of the following propositions did the *Dun & Bradstreet* Court establish?

(A) Gross negligence is required for the imposition of liability.

(B) Punitive damages may be awarded without any showing of fault.

(C) Strict liability may be imposed.

(D) Presumed damages, but not punitive damages, may be awarded in favor of private plaintiffs.

3.30. In *Hustler Magazine v. Falwell*, 485 U.S. 46 (1988), Hustler Magazine published an ad parody of the Reverend Jerry Falwell. The parody depicted Falwell having sex in an outhouse with his mother. Falwell sued, claiming that the Hustler ad involved the intentional infliction of emotional distress. In *Hustler Magazine*, the Court held that:

(A) Cases of intentional infliction of emotional distress should be treated differently than defamation cases for liability purposes (e.g., the actual malice standard does not apply).

(B) The actual malice standard should apply to cases alleging intentional infliction of mental and emotional distress.

(C) Strict liability can be imposed in intentional infliction cases.

(D) Simple negligence provides an adequate basis for damage awards in cases involving intentional infliction of emotional distress.

3.31. Please write a short essay explaining why *Hustler Magazine v. Falwell*, 485 U.S. 46 (1988), held that ad parodies are entitled to constitutional protection.

ANSWER:

3.32. Which statements about the constitutional standard for obscenity are true?

(A) The requirement that the material be "patently offensive" must be judged according to a national standard.

(B) Before someone can be convicted for exhibiting obscene materials, there must be a showing that the material has caused some harm to the community where the prosecution is taking place.

(C) Private possession of obscene material is constitutionally protected.

(D) The requirement that the material be "patently offensive" must be judged according to a local standard, unmodified by a national minimum of what is tolerable.

3.33. A bookstore in Jacksontown begins to stock a new bestselling book called *Sex Lives of the Rich and Famous*. The book is a collection of supposed first hand stories by movie stars, politicians and corporate tycoons, complete with photographs of models performing the activities described in the stories. While it is clear that most people are interested in the book because of its lascivious details and photographs that leave nothing to the imagination, some cultural commentators hail the book as a revealing window into America's obsession with celebrities. Indeed, the book gets nominated for several major book awards. The Jacksontown district attorney brings suit to declare the book obscene. A jury agrees, finding the book to aimed at the prurient interest and offensive. The bookstore appeals the judgment. Please explain whether the bookstore should win.

ANSWER:

3.34. Which of the following statements about the Supreme Court's definition of obscenity is correct?

(A) The requirement that a work lack "serious literary, artistic, political or scientific value" requires a judgment by a local jury, based on a local standard.

(B) The requirement that a work is "patently offensive" is made by a local jury, without any check by a reviewing court.

(C) The requirement that the work lack "serious literary, artistic, political or scientific value" means that any mention of literary, artistic, political or scientific issues in a work immunizes it from a government attempt to ban it.

(D) The requirement that a work lack "serious literary, artistic, political or scientific value" is made based on a national standard.

3.35. Which of the following statements best reflects the Supreme Court's historical approach to obscenity regulation?

(A) The Court has consistently held that obscenity lacks First Amendment protection.

(B) The Supreme Court has vacillated on the question whether obscenity lacks First Amendment protection.

(C) The Supreme Court has consistently held that obscenity enjoys First Amendment protection, although a lesser amount than the protection enjoyed by core political speech.

(D) The Supreme Court had previously held that obscenity lacked First Amendment protection, but has now settled on a view under which obscenity enjoys First Amendment protection, although a lesser amount than the protection enjoyed by core political speech.

3.36. Which of the following statements about obscenity (*not* including child pornography) is true?

(A) Government may prohibit its possession even in the home.

(B)   Government may not prohibit its possession in the home, but may prohibit its sale, distribution, and exhibition in public, even to interested and consenting parties.

(C)   Government may neither prohibit its possession in the home nor its sale, distribution, or exhibition in public, as long as that sale, distribution, or exhibition is to interested and consenting parties in a place shielded from the public at large.

(D)   Government may prohibit obscenity in any and all contexts.

4.1.   In the years since it decided *Chaplinsky v. New Hampshire*, 315 U.S. 568 (1942), the Supreme Court has held that other categories of speech (*e.g.*, child pornography) are not protected under the First Amendment to the United States Constitution. Which of the following statements is true regarding the Court's creation of these other categories of unprotected speech?

(A)   In creating these new categories of unprotected speech, the Court has consistently followed the *Chaplinsky* approach to categorical exclusions of speech.

(B)   With each excluded category of speech, the Court has focused solely on the speech value (*e.g.*, does it have only "slight value" towards ascertainment of the truth) of the particular category of speech.

(C)   In creating new categories of unprotected speech, the Court has sometimes focused on the societal interest in prohibiting the particular type of speech.

(D)   In creating these new categories of unprotected speech, the Court has explicitly rejected the *Chaplinsky* approach as outdated and inappropriate.

4.2.   Which of the following best describes the Supreme Court's current position regarding commercial speech?

(A)   The Court has recognized that commercial speech deserves some First Amendment protection, but that, given government's ability to regulate commercial transactions, government has substantial latitude to take the lesser step of restricting speech about those transactions.

(B)   The Court has officially elevated commercial speech to the same level of protection enjoyed by most other speech.

(C)   The Court has recognized that commercial speech deserves some First Amendment protection, and in recent years it has given more and more protection to such speech.

(D)   The Court has recognized that commercial speech deserves some First Amendment protection, but has given it the lowest level of protection.

4.3.   Which of the following has ***not*** been mentioned by the Supreme Court as a justification for according constitutional protection to commercial speech?

(A) Commercial speech allows consumers in a free market to make wise choices.

(B) Commercial speech speaks to issues citizens may care deeply about.

(C) Much speech that is traditionally thought to have been protected has been commercial in nature.

(D) Most of the underlying transactions that are the subject of commercial speech are constitutionally protected, thus making protection of the speech about them especially important.

4.4.   Which of the following statements about commercial speech is *incorrect*?

(A) For speech to be protected, it must not be misleading.

(B) Commercial speech has not always received First Amendment protection.

(C) Commercial speech restrictions are scrutinized under an intermediate scrutiny test.

(D) Commercial speech may be more readily restricted when government has the power to restrict the underlying transaction.

4.5.   Which of the following statements best describes the definition of commercial speech?

(A) Speech that proposes a commercial transaction.

(B) Speech made by a commercial entity for the ultimate purpose of earning money, regardless of whether it directly proposes a commercial transaction.

(C) Speech by a commercial entity.

(D) Paid advertisements ("commercials") on television or radio.

4.6.   Which of the following statements best describes the rules governing government restrictions on speech as a condition for government support?

(A) Government may not place any restrictions on speech as a condition for extending a government benefit.

(B) Government generally may not place restrictions on speech as a condition for getting a government benefit, but it may require that speech made through its own programs adopt a certain viewpoint.

(C) Government may place restrictions on speech as a condition for getting a government benefit, as long as the restriction is related to the benefit that is being conferred.

(D) Government may place any restriction it likes on speech as a condition for getting a government benefit, since the speaker can always turn down the benefit.

4.7. Utopia City enacts a statute that bans pornography "that demeans women or shows women as enjoying a submissive or subservient condition." Which of the following statements best indicates how a court would view such an ordinance?

(A) The statute might be upheld due to the harms such pornography is known to produce.

(B) The statute might be upheld as a valid time, place, and manner restriction on speech, in that it restricts the manner in which sexual activity is portrayed.

(C) The statute might be struck down as a content-based restriction on speech.

(D) The statute would be upheld in light of the lesser protection given sexual speech.

4.8. In order to ensure that children cannot access materials harmful to them, the federal government orders cable T.V. operators to block adult-oriented but non-obscene programming, with access granted only when a customer specifically requests it. How would a court analyze such a restriction?

(A) Because protection of children is a paramount government interest, the Court would probably review it under an intermediate scrutiny standard.

(B) Because it was a content-based restriction on speech, it would receive strict scrutiny.

(C) Because the restriction is on cable T.V., a medium that is marked by a scarcity of broadcast space, the restriction would get less than strict scrutiny.

(D) The government would lose if the plaintiff could prove that other means existed that would protect children equally.

4.9. The State of Jefferson restricts the sale of adult-oriented but non-obscene magazines to children, banning their sale to children unless accompanied by an adult. A child sues. How would the court analyze the child's claim?

(A) Since children are immature and generally thought to have no First Amendment rights, a court would easily uphold the restriction.

(B) Because children have the same First Amendment rights as adults, a court would analyze the claim as if it had been brought by an adult.

(C) Children have some First Amendment rights, but government has the right to protect them from inappropriate influences; thus, the court would probably uphold the restriction.

(D) Given the importance of free access to information, the Court would have to determine whether the particular child seeking the information had the maturity that would entitle him to that type of material.

4.10. Which of the following statements about campaign contributions best reflects the current state of the law?

(A) Campaign contributions are speech, and restrictions on contributions to a candidate's campaign are subject to the highest scrutiny.

(B) Campaign contributions are speech, but restrictions on that speech are subject to relatively deferential judicial scrutiny.

(C) Campaign contributions are not speech, and thus restrictions on them are not subject to First Amendment review at all.

(D) Campaign contributions are speech, but only when a candidate contributes to his own campaign.

4.11. The State of Utopia enacts a campaign finance law prohibiting any individual from spending more than $10,000 in direct expenditures in support of any particular candidate, defining "direct expenditure" to mean money spent on advertising or other media to promote the election of a particular candidate for office. A wealthy individual supporting a particular candidate sues, alleging that the law violates his First Amendment rights. What result?

(A) Just like contributions, direct expenditures are a marginal form of speech that receives only moderate judicial protection under the First Amendment.

(B) Unlike contributions, direct expenditures are at the core of the First Amendment's protection for political speech; thus, restrictions on such expenditures will receive strict scrutiny.

(C) Under the statute, direct expenditures involve only a commercial transaction — that is, the purchasing of advertising — and such expenditures receive only the protection accorded commercial speech.

(D) Direct expenditures are less protected speech than campaign contributions, and thus the Utopia statute would receive less judicial scrutiny than a restriction on campaign contributions.

4.12. Imagine now that, instead of restricting direct speech in the context of campaigns for electoral office, Utopia instead restricts direct expenditures in support of or opposition to a referendum campaign. How would a court analyze a First Amendment challenge to such a restriction?

(A) A court would probably impose something less than strict scrutiny, given the inherent differences between referendum and electoral campaigns.

(B) A court would probably impose even stricter scrutiny on direct expenditure limitations on referendum campaigns, given their relationship to direct democracy.

(C) A court would probably impose the same level of scrutiny on limitations of direct expenditures on referendum as on electoral campaigns.

(D) A court would probably find restrictions on direct expenditures on referendum campaigns to be constitutional.

4.13. In response to a particularly corrupt presidential election, Congress enacts a sweeping campaign finance law. Among other things, the law prohibits candidates from expending more than $100,000 on their own campaigns, prohibits individuals from contributing more than $10,000 to a campaign, and prohibits individuals from spending more than $50,000 for independent advertising for a particular candidate. Are these provisions constitutional?

ANSWER:

4.14. Under federal campaign finance law, if a candidate self-finances (*i.e.*, contributes a large dollar amount of his own money to his campaign), the candidate's opponent is freed from campaign finance restrictions up to the point where his contributions match the amount of the first candidate's self-financing. Max Millionaire, a wealthy candidate for a Senate seat, self-finances his campaign. When Paul Poorguy, his opponent, starts accepting large campaign contributions in excess of what the law would normally allow Poorguy to collect, Millionaire sues, alleging a violation of his First Amendment rights. What result?

(A) Millionaire wins: the law burdens his ability to spend money on behalf of his own candidacy by making that spending a trigger for his opponent being able to collect more in contributions.

(B) Millionaire wins: any law restricting campaign contributions and spending is unconstitutional unless narrowly tailored to further a compelling government interest, a test that has never been met in the campaign finance context.

(C) Millionaire loses: the law does not restrict what Millionaire can spend on his own campaign but rather just helps ensure that his opponent is capable of matching a self-financing candidate's expenditures.

(D) Millionaire loses: while restrictions on campaign contributions may be unconstitutional, restrictions on campaign spending are generally allowed.

4.15. Assume instead that Utopia enacts a law restricting any corporation from spending more than $10,000 in direct expenditures on any political campaign, but allowing unlimited corporate expenditures as long as the funds come from a fund made up of voluntary contributions, rather than general corporate funds. Should the statute be upheld?

(A) Because direct expenditures enjoy such a high degree of constitutional protection, the statute would probably be struck down.

(B) Because direct expenditures do not enjoy a particularly high degree of constitutional protection, the statute would probably be upheld.

(C) Because of the special circumstances surrounding the accumulation of capital in the corporate form, the statute would probably be upheld.

(D) Because of the special circumstances surrounding the accumulation of capital in the corporate form, the statute would probably be struck down.

4.16. Utopia's constitution allows referendums to be placed on the ballot if a number of voters equal to 10% of the turnout in the last general election sign a petition to that effect. Suppose that Utopia becomes concerned that large corporations are effectively hijacking the state's initiative and referendum process, by paying large sums of money in order to gather voter signatures to place a referendum on the ballot. According to Utopia's legislature, this phenomenon undermines the grassroots nature of the referendum process. What restrictions on the referendum process would be most likely to be upheld?

(A) Utopia could require that the petition signature gatherers not be paid, in order to preserve their volunteer, grassroots status.

(B) Utopia could require that petition signature gatherers be identified by wearing a name plate.

(C) Utopia could require that the petition signature gatherers be registered voters in Utopia.

(D) Utopia could require that sponsors of ballot initiatives disclose who paid for the petition signature gatherers.

4.17. Which of the following statements is not a part of current First Amendment doctrine regarding restrictions on campaign contributions?

(A) Government has a legitimate interest in curbing not just the reality but the perception that moneyed interest can corrupt the political process.

(B) Government has a legitimate interest in restricting the speech of some in order to balance the speech on either side of a political issue.

(C) Direct expenditures in support of a political candidate enjoy significant First Amendment protections.

(D) Corporations have at least some rights to influence the political process, even though corporations cannot vote.

4.18. Which of the following statements best reflects the Court's approach to the freedom of speech enjoyed by government employees?

(A) The Court balances the individual's interest in free speech with the government's interest in the efficient provision of the services provided by the employee.

(B) Because of the custodial nature of the government's role, the government has the same broad power to restrict employee speech just as private employers do.

(C) Government employees lose none of their First Amendment rights when they enter the government workplace.

(D) The public importance of the subject of the employee's speech is irrelevant to the analysis, since the question is the individual's right to speak on what topic he or she wishes.

4.19. The district attorney's office in Mountainville is in an uproar. One of the attorneys in the office, after being denied a promotion, distributed an internal memorandum highly critical of the way promotion decisions are made. While respectful in tone, the memo calls attention to several promotion-related issues that it asserts are causing a serious morale problem in the office, and solicits other office attorneys' views on the matters. The attorney is fired for insubordination, and in turn brings suit, alleging violations of the First Amendment. How should the lawsuit be resolved?

ANSWER:

4.20. Assume that, upon hearing of the attempted assassination of the President, a civilian employee of a local sheriff's department is heard to say, while he is on duty at the station house, "If they come after him again I hope they get him; otherwise he'll ruin this country." The employee is fired and sues, alleging deprivation of his First Amendment rights. How would a court analyze the employee's First Amendment claim?

(A) Because such statements are inherently out of order in the context of a law enforcement agency, the employee would lose his claim.

(B) Because the statement touched on a matter of public interest, the employee would have a good First Amendment claim unless the government could show that the context of the statements was such that they impeded the efficient functioning of the sheriff's office.

(C) Because such statements touch on core political issues, they would necessarily be protected.

    (D)   Because one has a right to speak but no right to government employment, the employee would lose his First Amendment claim.

4.21.   The City of Mount Pretty decides to deal with the proliferation of adult bookstores and theaters in town by requiring that they be concentrated in a three-square-block area east of downtown. The owner of an adult bookstore located in a residential area north of downtown sues, alleging that the restriction violates his First Amendment rights. He alleges that relatively few locations in the area reserved for such speech are suitable for business, and that it would be expensive to relocate and to create a space suitable for his business in that area. Assuming that fact to be true, does the bookstore owner have a good First Amendment claim?

ANSWER:

4.22.   In response to complaints from residents, the city of Big Falls enacts an ordinance requiring that, after 10:00 p.m. on weekdays and midnight on weekends, bar owners maintain an outside noise level of 60 decibels or below (you can assume that 60 decibels is the level at which most live music is performed). Frank Furious, owner of Frank's Furious Lounge, brings suit claiming that the hard rock bands he books would not be able to perform at their customary noise level if they were required to comply with that ordinance. Does he have a good First Amendment claim?

ANSWER:

4.23.   The International Society for a New Consciousness (ISNC) is a religious sect that believes in soliciting money from strangers in order to fund its meditation activities. Members of the group go to Chicago's O'Hare airport, which is owned by the City of Chicago, to solicit such funds. They are told they must stop that activity, due to a city ordinance that bans solicitation at the airport. ISNC brings suit, claiming that the restriction violates the First Amendment. Does ISNC have a good First Amendment claim?

ANSWER:

4.24.   In *Virginia v. Black*, 538 U.S. 343 (2003), the United States Supreme Court issued a landmark decision on the subject of cross burning. Which of the following statements correctly summarizes *Black's* holding?

    (A)   Cross burning can be prohibited when it is conducted with the intent to intimidate another person.

    (B)   Because it is so pernicious, cross burning can be prohibited under all circumstances.

(C) Because the cross is regarded as a sacred religious symbol, government has an absolute right to prohibit individuals from burning crosses in a desecrating manner.

(D) Cross burning can never be prohibited.

5.1.   Which of the following statements is true?

   (A) Government has the greatest latitude to restrict speech on government-owned property it uses for its own purposes and on private property; it has the least latitude to restrict speech on government-owned property that is designed for speech or which has historically been used for that purpose.

   (B) Government has the greatest latitude to restrict speech on government-owned property it uses for its own purposes; restrictions on speech on private property are scrutinized more carefully.

   (C) Government has equal latitude to restrict speech on any property that it owns.

   (D) Government has the greatest latitude to restrict speech on private property, and the least latitude to restrict speech on its own property.

5.2.   Which of the following statements about the Court's public forum analysis is correct?

   (A) The Court recognizes as public forums both areas traditionally opened to speech activities and those explicitly dedicated to such activities.

   (B) The Court recognizes an ever-expanding universe of traditional public forums, as new ways of social interaction make new areas, such as airports, the hubs of much public social interaction.

   (C) In order for an area to be a non-public forum, it must be one that citizens other than employees are not allowed to enter.

   (D) Public forums are defined as areas that are necessary, because of their unique characteristics, for a given type of speech to be fully effective.

5.3.   The Rockland Chapter of the Fraternal Order of Hawks donates to the City of Rockland a sculpture depicting the first settlers coming into Rockland. The City accepts the donation and places the sculpture in a city-owned park, where it sits with a number of other large sculptures. A group of Native Americans then asks the city for permission to place a similar-sized sculpture showing members of the native tribe that lived in Rockland before the settlers arrived. The city denies the request. The tribe sues, alleging that the park is a public forum and that the city's denial represents a content- or viewpoint-based restriction on speech. What result?

(A) The denial is a content-based restriction that would be subject to strict scrutiny.

(B) The denial is a content-based restriction and therefore would be subject to a deferential balancing test.

(C) The denial is not a content-based restriction because placement of donated monuments in a park constitutes government speech, rather than the speech of the donating party. Because it is government speech, the content-neutrality requirement does not apply.

(D) The denial is not a content-based restriction because any speech that happens on government property is necessarily government speech.

5.4. The City of Washington, D.C., enacts an ordinance both (1) prohibiting the display of signs criticizing a foreign government on any sidewalk within 1,000 feet of its embassy, and (2) allowing police to disperse crowds gathering on any sidewalk within 1,000 feet of an embassy if there is a threat to security. Are these provisions constitutional?

(A) Neither provision would be constitutional because they both restrict speech on traditional public forums.

(B) The ban on sign displays would be unconstitutional, but the authorization to disperse crowds might survive a constitutional challenge.

(C) Both provisions would be constitutional because they further the legitimate interest of promoting good relations with foreign nations.

(D) Both provisions would be constitutional because sidewalks historically have been dedicated to public transit rather than speech.

5.5. Andy Activist wishes to hand out political leaflets. After studying his town, he decides that the best place to distribute the leaflets is at the local shopping mall. The downtown shopping area of the town has largely disappeared due to the mall, and a large percentage of the town's population goes to the mall to do their shopping, as well as to stroll down the center of the mall itself, which has functionally become the town's main strolling area. After the mall manager ejects Andy, he brings suit, claiming that his First Amendment rights have been violated. Will Andy win or lose his lawsuit?

(A) Andy loses: the Supreme Court has never held that private property has to be opened to speech with which the property owner disagrees.

(B) Andy loses: although the Supreme Court at times has indicated that privately-owned shopping areas can be subjected to the First Amendment, the Court has since cut back on that jurisprudence to the point that only company-owned towns can be subjected to the First Amendment.

(C) Andy wins if he can show that most residents of the town do in fact view the shopping mall as their main shopping and strolling area.

(D) Andy wins: the First Amendment applies to speech in shopping malls.

5.6. During a tightly contested city election, one candidate's campaign seeks to operate a sound truck through the city around the clock, broadcasting the candidate's message. The City informs the campaign that a city ordinance prohibits the use of sound trucks between 8pm and 8am. The campaign sues, claiming an infringement on free speech. Will the campaign win or lose its lawsuit?

(A) The campaign wins, since the speech at issue is core political speech entitled to full First Amendment protection.

(B) The campaign loses, since the restriction is probably a valid time, place, and manner regulation.

(C) The campaign wins, since time, place and manner regulations are usually valid but not when they have the effect of squelching speech on matters of great public interest.

(D) The campaign loses, since campaign finance laws that have been held constitutional have allowed restrictions on this type of speech.

5.7. Which of the following statements about time, place, and manner restrictions on speech is true?

(A) They must be narrowly tailored to achieve the government's interest, which in practice has meant that such restrictions are scrutinized very closely.

(B) The fact that they must be content-neutral means that the Court's ends-means scrutiny is relatively deferential.

(C) They must be content-neutral, but they cannot be viewpoint-neutral.

(D) They cannot be content- or viewpoint-neutral.

5.8. The State of Xenophobia enacts a law prohibiting the burning of an American flag except when necessary to destroy a damaged flag, in accordance with military regulations governing the respectful destruction of a damaged flag. The statute states that it is enacted in order "to protect and show respect for fundamental American values of patriotism and love of country, and to show respect for those who fought and died in the nation's wars." During a political protest, a protester burns an American flag and is arrested. Can he be validly convicted for violating the statute?

(A)   NO. The statute clearly bans flag burning except when done in a way respectful to it; this makes it a viewpoint-based restriction on speech.

(B)   YES. Given the special place the flag has in American life, a state may prescribe special rules for its respect and protection.

(C)   YES. Burning a flag is not speech and thus does not come within the protections of the First Amendment.

(D)   NO. Because any flag-burning statute restricts the speech implicit in burning a flag, the statute is unconstitutional.

5.9.   In late December of a given year, the Chicago Times, a major newspaper, obtains secret information that a terrorist group is planning to attack Chicago with a nuclear device on New Year's Day. In order to avert a panic, the government sues to have a court enjoin publication of that information. Should the court enjoin publication?

(A)   The court should enjoin publication if the government can prove that publication of the information will seriously injure the national interest.

(B)   The court should enjoin the publication only in the very rarest of cases, and the government will have an extraordinarily high hurdle to surmount.

(C)   The court should enjoin publication if the government can prove that the information has been obtained illegally, and thus represented illegal conduct by the newspaper.

(D)   The court should never enjoin publication.

5.10.   The City of Rocktown enacts an ordinance requiring that all adult-oriented theaters (showing sexual, but non-obscene movies) be located at least a mile away from each other, and at least half a mile away from any church or school. The ordinance states that the purpose of the action is to prevent the congregating of such businesses into a "red light district," which, according to the ordinance, would cause public drunkenness, prostitution, and other crimes. Sid Sleazy, owner of a three such theaters in Rocktown, brings suit, claiming that the ordinance violates the First Amendment. One of his allegations, which you can accept as true, is that the characteristics of land use and the real estate market in Rocktown are such that, given the ordinance, Sid will not be able to find an adequate parcel on which to erect a theater. Should Sid win his lawsuit?

(A)   Sid probably wins. Because the ordinance singles out theaters that show adult films, it is content-based and will be subject to strict scrutiny, which the ordinance would probably fail.

(B) Sid probably loses. Because the ordinance cites non-speech related concerns, it will probably be held to a more lenient test for speech that is restricted in the pursuit of ameliorating the secondary effects of that speech.

(C) Sid probably wins, because the ordinance's operation makes it very difficult for Sid to speak through his operation of the theaters.

(D) Sid probably loses because such speech enjoys no constitutional protection.

5.11. The City of Prudetown bans nude dancing, on the ground that it is injurious to the public morals and causes a variety of social harms such as prostitution and drunkenness. The ordinance says nothing about other forms of nudity. Could the ordinance survive First Amendment scrutiny?

(A) Probably, since a majority of the Supreme Court would be willing either to defer to the city's judgment that nude dancing caused prostitution and drunkenness, or to allow the city to regulate based on a concern for public morals.

(B) Probably not, since by restricting nude dancing but not other nudity, the city was engaging in a content-based restriction on the symbolic speech of dancing.

(C) Probably, since dancing would not be considered speech and thus would not receive First Amendment protection.

(D) Probably not, since the ordinance, by restricting all nude dancing, allowed no avenue for the unique expression that is nude dancing.

5.12. During a protest march against United States involvement in a war in the Middle East, Peter Protester gets on a stage, douses his draft-eligibility card in oil, and sets it on fire. He is arrested and charged with intentional destruction of his draft card, a federal offense. He defends based on the First Amendment. Should Peter win or lose the lawsuit?

(A) Peter wins, since he was clearly burning his draft card in order to express his opposition to the war.

(B) Peter loses, since his act was conduct, not speech, and thus unprotected by the First Amendment.

(C) Peter loses, unless he can prove that his action was sincerely motivated by a desire to express his opposition to the war, and not simply by a desire to break the law.

(D) Peter loses if the government can show that it had a legitimate, non-speech related reason for the law, and if it can show that there was no less speech-restrictive way of furthering that interest.

5.13. Which of the following statements regarding the vagueness doctrine is incorrect?

(A) Vague laws fail to give adequate notice to those subject to the law, and accordingly fail to give them an opportunity to comply with the law.

(B) Vague laws are objectionable because they vest arbitrary and discriminatory enforcement power in administrators.

(C) The doctrine has special force as applied to laws affecting free speech.

(D) Vague laws are inherently invalid in every area of the law.

5.14. In general, the Court requires litigants to bring "as applied" rather than "facial" challenges to overbroad laws. Which of the following is *not* a justification for this rule?

(A) By focusing on the facts before the court, the case focuses on "flesh and blood" issues rather than abstract principles.

(B) Court rules absolutely preclude consideration of "facial" challenges.

(C) As a general rule, litigants are not allowed to raise the rights of others not before the court.

(D) "As applied" challenges are more consistent with the judicial function.

5.15. As a precondition to applying the overbreadth doctrine, the Court requires a showing of:

(A) "Some overbreadth."

(B) "Any overbreadth."

(C) "Substantial overbreadth."

(D) "Great overbreadth."

5.16. Please explain the underpinnings of the vagueness doctrine.
ANSWER:

5.17. Please describe the concept of "prior restraint."
ANSWER:

5.18. Please describe the concept of "licensing" as it applies to "prior restraints."
ANSWER:

5.19.   In *Lovell v. City of Griffin*, 303 U.S. 444 (1938), the Court was confronted by a Griffin, Georgia, ordinance which made it illegal to distribute, among other things, literature and circulars without a license. The Court held that:

(A)   The ordinance was constitutional because states, through their police powers, have an interest in controlling the distribution of literature.

(B)   The ordinance was constitutional because it was narrowly tailored.

(C)   The ordinance was invalid on its face as a prior restraint.

(D)   In evaluating the ordinance, a reviewing court must weigh the local interest against the interest in free speech.

5.20.   Which of the following is ***not*** an accurate description of the Court's conclusions in *Lovell v. City of Griffin*, 303 U.S. 444 (1938), which dealt with an ordinance requiring a license before distributing literature in the city?

(A)   The ordinance involved an example of censorship and licensing in its baldest form.

(B)   The ordinance strikes at the very foundation of freedom of the press by subjecting literature and circulars to censorship.

(C)   Freedom of the press is not limited to newspapers, but extends to pamphlets and circulars.

(D)   Freedom of the press extends to newspapers, but not to pamphlets and circulars.

5.21.   Under the prohibition against prior restraints, courts generally state that:

(A)   All licensing restrictions on speech are inherently unconstitutional.

(B)   Licensing restrictions on speech will sometimes be upheld when they involve content-neutral time, place, and manner restrictions.

(C)   Licensing restraints on speech will only be upheld when they are supported by a "compelling governmental interest."

(D)   Licensing restraints are exempt from the prior restraint doctrine.

5.22.   In *Freedman v. Maryland*, 380 U.S. 51 (1965), the Court held that a licensing scheme for motion pictures could be upheld only if certain conditions were met. Which of the following is one of those conditions?

(A)   The burden of proving that the film constitutes unprotected expression must rest with the censor or licensor.

(B)   Within a specified period of time, the censor must either issue a license or go to court to seek an order against exhibiting the film.

(C)   A court must have the final decision whether to censor a film.

(D)   All of these were identified in *Freedman* as necessary conditions for a valid film licensing scheme.

5.23.   In *Bantam Books, Inc. v. Sullivan*, 372 U.S. 58 (1963), the Court confronted a law under which a state advised booksellers that certain books were objectionable, for corrupting young people. Which of the following correctly states how the Court analyzed the law?

(A)   The fact that the law merely advised booksellers of the state's view meant that there was no legal sanction for selling them, and thus, no First Amendment violation.

(B)   The state's special interest in protecting youth justified any coercion implicit in the state's action.

(C)   The state's actions amounted to an unconstitutional prior restraint.

(D)   There was no state action since the bookseller refrained from selling the books on his own initiative, after receiving the state's list.

5.24.   *Kingsley International Pictures Corp. v. Regents*, 360 U.S. 684 (1959), involved a New York statute that allowed censors to refuse to license any film that contained material that was "obscene, indecent, immoral, inhuman, sacrilegious, or [was] of such a character that its exhibition would tend to corrupt morals or incite to [crime]." Appellant's application for a license to distribute *Lady Chatterley's Lover* was denied on the basis that the film was immoral because it presented adultery as a "desirable, acceptable, and proper pattern of behavior." The Court held that:

(A)   The denial was proper because such material is immoral and unsuitable for children.

(B)   The denial was unconstitutional because it improperly censored an idea (the notion that adultery is a "desirable, acceptable, and proper" form of behavior).

(C)   The denial was proper because, under its police power, the state has the right to prohibit dangerous ideas relating to such things as adultery.

(D)   The denial was proper because ideas relating to adultery are not protected.

5.25.   *Near v. Minnesota*, 283 U.S. 697 (1931), involved a Minnesota statute that allowed the county attorneys to seek abatement of public nuisances including any publication that is "malicious, scandalous, or defamatory." The *Saturday Press* ran a series of viciously anti-Semitic articles making allegations about a

"Jewish gangster" influence and local government corruption. The local county attorney sought and obtained an injunction against the newspaper. In *Near*, the Court held that:

(A) Even though prior restraints are disfavored, injunctions against newspapers that publish "malicious, scandalous, and defamatory" material are permissible.

(B) An injunction against a newspaper is permissible if it is issued by a court rather than by an administrative official.

(C) Injunctions against newspapers are permissible when the newspaper is being operated as a "public nuisance."

(D) Prior restraints against newspapers are presumptively unconstitutional.

5.26. Describe the facts and the *per curiam* holding in *New York Times Co. v. United States*, 403 U.S. 713 (1971) (the "Pentagon Papers" case).

ANSWER:

5.27. *Madsen v. Women's Health Center, Inc.*, 512 U.S. 753 (1994), involved a lower-court injunction against protestors at an abortion clinic. When the protestors violated the injunction, the court imposed additional restrictions on the protestors. In reviewing the injunction, the United States Supreme Court held that:

(A) Injunctions, like other prior restraints, should be subject to strict scrutiny.

(B) In evaluating injunctions, courts must ask whether the challenged provisions of the injunction burden no more speech than necessary to serve a significant government interest.

(C) Injunctions, since they are issued by judges, are subject to only rational basis review.

(D) Injunctions against abortion protestors should be evaluated as content-based and viewpoint-based restrictions on speech.

5.28. In *Madsen v. Women's Health Center, Inc.*, 512 U.S. 753 (1994), the Court was confronted by a lower-court injunction against abortion protestors. In analyzing the statute, the Court was confronted by arguments that the injunction was not content-neutral, and therefore ran afoul of the Court's prior holding in *R.A.V. v. St. Paul*, 505 U.S. 377, 386 (1992) ("The government may not regulate [speech] based on hostility — or favoritism — towards the underlying message expressed"). What did the Court hold in *Madsen*?

(A) The injunction was a content-based restriction on the abortion protestor's speech.

(B)   The injunction was a viewpoint-based restriction on the abortion protestor's speech.

(C)   The mere fact that the injunction covered people with a particular viewpoint did not itself render the injunction content- or viewpoint-based.

(D)   The injunction was both a content-based and a viewpoint-based restriction on the abortion protestor's speech.

5.29. Which of the following statements accurately reflects the law concerning conduct that has expressive content?

(A)   Because all conduct can be thought to express some message, conduct has no special First Amendment protection.

(B)   Because some conduct is highly expressive, government must show that restrictions on such conduct are not motivated by a desire to suppress that expression.

(C)   Because all conduct can be thought to express some message, the First Amendment prohibits government from suppressing any conduct that expresses a message.

(D)   Conduct that expresses a message can only be suppressed if government has a rational basis for doing so.

6.1.   Discuss the various views about whether the press should be granted a "preferred" or "privileged" position under the First Amendment.

ANSWER:

6.2.   In *Branzburg v. Hayes*, 408 U.S. 665 (1972), a reporter was subpoenaed to testify in an ongoing criminal case. He refused to testify on the ground that the testimony would force him to reveal his sources, and therefore would compromise his future efforts to report. In essence, he claimed that the subpoena violated the First Amendment. In *Branzburg*, the Court:

   (A)   Accepted the reporter's refusal to testify on the ground that the First Amendment gives reporters an absolute right to refuse to reveal their sources.

   (B)   Accepted the reporter's refusal to testify on the ground that a refusal to recognize a reporter's First Amendment privilege would undermine the freedom of the press to collect and disseminate news.

   (C)   Refused to allow the reporter to decline to testify, reasoning that the public interest in investigating crime outweighs the reporter's interest in preventing disclosure.

   (D)   Refused to allow the reporter to decline to testify, reasoning that reporters are not protected under the First Amendment

6.3.   *Cohen v. Cowles Media Co.*, 501 U.S. 663 (1991), involved a reporter who gave a source a promise of confidentiality in exchange for information. When the reporter breached the promise, the source sued the reporter for damages. In *Cowles*, the Court held that:

   (A)   The First Amendment prevents a reporter from being sued for breaching a promise of confidentiality to a source.

   (B)   The First Amendment does not preclude a reporter from being sued for breaching a promise of confidentiality to a source because it is no more than the incidental consequence of applying to the press a generally applicable law that requires those who make certain kinds of promises to keep them.

(C) The First Amendment prevents a reporter from being sued for breaching a promise of confidentiality to a source absent a showing of "actual malice" in the reporter's decision to breach.

(D) The First Amendment exempts reporters from general contract law when performing their newsgathering functions.

6.4. *Zurcher v. Stanford Daily*, 436 U.S. 547 (1978), involved a disturbance on Stanford University's campus in which policemen were assaulted. Following the incident, the *Stanford Daily* published an article about the incident which was accompanied by photographs. The article suggested that the *Daily*'s reporter was in a position where he could have seen and photographed the assault on the police. Based on the *Daily* article, the police obtained a search warrant for photographs and other information in the newspaper's offices that might identify the perpetrators. The *Daily* sued claiming, *inter alia*, an infringement of its First Amendment rights. In *Zurcher*, the Court held that:

(A) The search warrant was not *per se* invalid under the First and Fourth Amendments to the United States Constitution.

(B) The First Amendment absolutely prohibits the police from obtaining search warrants authorizing intrusion into newspaper offices.

(C) Although the First Amendment prohibits the police from obtaining search warrants authorizing intrusion into public offices, it does authorize a *subpoena duces tecum*.

(D) Search warrants should not issue against news organizations unless reviewed by an appellate court for consistency with the First Amendment.

6.5. In *Globe Newspaper Co. v. Superior Court*, 457 U.S. 596 (1982), a Massachusetts law required the exclusion of the press and the public from courtrooms during the testimony of victims of certain sexual offenses who were under the age of 18. In *Globe*, the Court held that:

(A) The state had a compelling governmental interest in protecting the minor victims of sexual offenses, and that interest justified the closure law.

(B) The state had a compelling governmental interest in protecting the minor victims of sexual offenses, but that interest could be served through case-by-case closure decisions that honored First Amendment interests to the maximum extent possible.

(C) When the state interest in protecting minors is balanced against the press and the public's interest in attending the trial, the First Amendment never mandates press admission, which is solely a matter of judicial discretion.

(D) The press has no right of access to judicial proceedings.

6.6.　Please write a short answer explaining why, in *Globe Newspaper v. Superior Court*, 457 U.S. 596 (1982), the Court held that criminal trials should generally be open to the public.

ANSWER:

6.7.　*Press-Enterprise Co. v. Superior Court*, 478 U.S. 1 (1986), involved a request for access to the transcript of a preliminary hearing (which the Court compared in importance to a trial itself) in a murder case. The defendant moved for exclusion of the press, and the motion was granted in an effort to ensure that the defendant received a fair trial. When the hearing was over, a newspaper asked for a transcript of the hearing. The judge refused to grant the request and sealed the record. In *Press-Enterprise*, the Court held that:

(A) A trial court judge may deny press access to the transcript of a preliminary hearing if that action is "reasonably necessary" to protect defendant's right to a fair trial.

(B) The defendant has a constitutional right to demand that a preliminary hearing be closed and that the transcript be sealed.

(C) The press and the public have a constitutional right of access to preliminary hearings (and the transcripts of those hearings), which can only be overcome is there is a "substantial probability" of prejudice to the defendant's fair trial rights and there is no other way to mitigate that prejudice.

(D) The press has no right of access to transcripts.

6.8.　In *Chandler v. Florida*, 449 U.S. 560 (1981), a trial court provided for radio, television, and still photographic coverage of a criminal trial for public broadcast, notwithstanding the objection of the accused. In reviewing the lower court ruling, the United States Supreme Court held that:

(A) A trial court may not allow radio, television, and still photographic coverage of a trial over the accused's objections.

(B) A trial court has free rein to permit radio, television, and still photographic coverage without regard to an accused's objections.

(C) A trial court's decision to permit radio, television, and still photographic coverage without regard to an accused's objections is permissible provided that the fairness of the accused's trial is not compromised.

(D) Radio and television reporters must be excluded from all judicial proceedings.

6.9.　In *Pell v. Procunier*, 417 U.S. 817 (1974), news organizations challenged a California Department of Corrections regulation which precluded press and media interviews with prison inmates. In *Pell*, the Court held that:

(A) The press does not have a constitutional right of special access to information not available to the public generally.

(B) Inmates, like other citizens, have a First Amendment right to free speech, which includes the right to do interviews with the media.

(C) The media has a First Amendment right to interview prison inmates.

(D) The First Amendment has no application in the prison context.

6.10. In *Sheppard v. Maxwell*, 384 U.S. 333 (1966), Sheppard was convicted of murdering his wife after extensive pre-trial publicity, and extensive coverage during the trial itself. In *Sheppard*, the Supreme Court rendered the following ruling in reviewing Sheppard's conviction on a habeas petition:

(A) The petition should be denied because Sheppard received a fair trial notwithstanding the publicity.

(B) The petition should be granted because the state trial judge did not fulfill his duty to protect Sheppard from the inherently prejudicial publicity which saturated the community.

(C) The petition should be granted because the trial court's failure to enter a gag order prohibiting all pretrial publicity denied the defendant a fair trial.

(D) The petition should be denied because defendants do not have a constitutional right to restricted trial publicity.

6.11. In a case like *Sheppard v. Maxwell*, 384 U.S. 333 (1966), in which the Court is faced by extensive pretrial publicity, what steps might the trial court have taken to ensure that defendant received a fair trial?

ANSWER:

7.1.   Over the course of history, new forms of technology have developed and the courts (and, sometimes, legislatures) have been forced to decide how to handle that technology in terms of legal analysis. Under cases like *Lovell v. City of Griffin*, 303 U.S. 444 (1938), and *Near v. Minnesota*, 283 U.S. 697 (1931), the Court has provided strong First Amendment protection to traditional media like books and newspapers. In *Red Lion Broadcasting Co. v. FCC*, 395 U.S. 367 (1969), the Court was forced to decide how the broadcast media (radio and television) should be treated for First Amendment purposes. In *Red Lion*, the Court held that broadcast media should be treated:

(A)   Like newspapers and books in that it receives broad First Amendment protections.

(B)   Differently than books and newspapers because broadcast media is different than books and newspapers.

(C)   As deserving of no First Amendment protection whatsoever.

(D)   As deserving of more protection than books and newspapers because of its communicative potential.

7.2.   Please explain why, in *Red Lion Broadcasting Co. v. FCC*, 395 U.S. 367 (1969), the Court decided to treat the broadcast media differently than books and newspapers for First Amendment purposes.

ANSWER:

7.3.   In *Red Lion Broadcasting Co. v. FCC*, 395 U.S. 367 (1969), the Court considered application of FCC rules to radio broadcasters. Which of the following rules was upheld in that case?

(A)   The "multiple ownership" rule, which precludes broadcasters from owning more than one media outlet.

(B)   The "After 10:00 p.m." rule, which requires broadcasters to broadcast "indecent" material only after 10:00 p.m.

(C) The "fairness doctrine," which requires broadcasters to give adequate coverage to public issues and to make sure that coverage is "fair" in that it reflects opposing views.

(D) The "Children's Programming" rule, which requires broadcasters to air a minimum of three hours of children's programming per day.

7.4. *FCC v. Pacifica Foundation*, 438 U.S. 726 (1978), involved a comedian's monologue, known as "Filthy Words," filled with profanity that was aired on a broadcast radio station during the daytime as part of a program on contemporary attitudes towards language. When the broadcaster challenged the FCC's order finding an administrative violation in the airing of the program, the United States Supreme Court held that:

(A) Content such as the "Filthy Words" monologue can be banned from the airwaves.

(B) The FCC can require content such as the "Filthy Words" monologue to be "channeled" to times (*e.g.*, late at night) when children were less likely to be listening.

(C) Radio stations have an absolute right to air any content, including those such as the "Filthy Words" monologue.

(D) Content such as the "Filthy Words" monologue can be broadcast, even during daylight hours, because those who are offended can simply switch stations.

7.5. *Turner Broadcasting System, Inc. v. FCC*, 520 U.S. 180 (1997) (*Turner II*), and *Turner Broadcasting v. FCC*, 512 U.S. 622 (1994) (*Turner I*), both involved a federal statute that required cable companies to devote a portion of their channels to the broadcast of local television stations. Cable stations challenged this so-called "must carry" rule as an infringement of their First Amendment rights. What of the following statements best reflects First Amendment law after the *Turner Broadcasting* cases?

(A) Cable companies have an absolute right to decide what they broadcast on their channels.

(B) If a sufficient governmental interest can be shown, cable companies can be required to devote a portion of their channels to the broadcast of local stations.

(C) Cable companies can be required to devote a portion of their channels to the broadcast of local stations, but only if this "taking" of their property is accompanied by just compensation.

(D) Cable companies have a constitutional right to exclude local stations.

7.6. In *Denver Area Educational Telecommunications Consortium, Inc. v. FCC*, 518

U.S. 727 (1996), the Court was confronted by the Cable Television Consumer Protection and Competition Act of 1992, which regulated the broadcasting of "patently offensive," sex-related material on cable television. The Act applied to programs broadcast over cable on what are known as "leased access channels" and "public, educational, or governmental channels." These channels carry programs provided by those to whom the law gives special cable system access rights.

The Act contained three provisions. Section 10(a) allowed cable system operators to prohibit the broadcasting of "programming" that the "operator reasonably believes describes or depicts sexual or excretory activities or organs in a patently offensive manner" over "leased access" channels. Section 10(c) allowed cable operators to impose similar restrictions over public access channels. The remaining provision required cable system operators to segregate certain "patently offensive" programming, to place it on a single channel, and to block that channel from viewer access unless the viewer requests access in advance and in writing.

Which of these provisions were upheld in *Denver Area*?

(A) § 10(a) (which allowed cable system operators to prohibit the broadcasting of "programming" that the "operator reasonably believes describes or depicts sexual or excretory activities or organs in a patently offensive manner" over "leased access" channels).

(B) § 10(c) (which was similar to § 10(a), but provided for similar restrictions on public access channels).

(C) The remaining provision (which required cable system operators to segregate certain "patently offensive" programming, to place it on a single channel, and to block that channel from viewer access unless the viewer requests access in advance and in writing).

(D) Only § 10(a) and § 10(c).

7.7. *Reno v. American Civil Liberties Union*, 521 U.S. 844 (1997), involved the Communications Decency Act, which was designed to protect minors from "indecent" and "patently offensive" material on the Internet. The *Reno* Court held that:

(A) Speech on the Internet enjoys the same level of First Amendment protection as broadcasting.

(B) The government has a right to control content on the Internet in pursuit of its goal of increasing Internet usage by minimizing the chance of users encountering offensive material.

(C) Speech on the Internet enjoys full constitutional protection.

(D) The government can ban "indecent" and "patently offensive" content from the Internet, but only if it can satisfy the intermediate scrutiny necessary to justify content-based restrictions on Internet speech.

7.8.   Please discuss whether the Internet should be treated like broadcast regulation in terms of the government's ability to impose restrictions on speech engaged in via that medium.

ANSWER:

7.9.   In the "Children's Internet Protection Act" (CIPA), Congress prohibits the commercial displays on the World Wide Web of "sexual material that is harmful to minors." (Assume that the definition of the restricted material excludes child pornography, which is regulated in a separate statute.) A coalition of online pornography websites sues and seeks a preliminary injunction, alleging that the statute is overbroad and thus likely unconstitutional. What is the likely result?

(A) The plaintiffs will likely lose: the fact that the speech is occurring on the Internet means that it will get less protection and will not be subject to the type of scrutiny that would require restrictions not to be overbroad.

(B) The plaintiffs will likely lose: even though speech on the Internet gets full First Amendment protection, the fact that the speech at issue here is harmful to minors means that restrictions on that speech will be reviewed deferentially.

(C) The plaintiffs would likely win as long as they could prove that user-provided filtering software would likely be effective in preventing minors from accessing this material.

(D) The plaintiffs would likely win unless the government could prove that user-provided filtering software would likely be ineffective in preventing minors from accessing this material.

7.10.   Which of the following is not currently a relevant consideration when considering the scope of Congress' ability to regulate the broadcast media?

(A) The pervasiveness of the medium subject to the regulation.

(B) The ease with which children could access that medium unsupervised by adults.

(C) The usefulness of the medium for facilitating broad-ranging speech.

(D) The conclusion that, based on history, the broadcast medium is not entitled to constitutional protection.

8.1.   In *NAACP v. Alabama*, 357 U.S. 449 (1958), and other cases, the United States Supreme Court has recognized a right to freedom of association. In *NAACP*, the Court relied on which of the following considerations as underlying that right?

   (A) Effective advocacy of both public and private points of view, particularly controversial ones — and thus, effective use of the right of free speech — is undeniably enhanced by group association.

   (B) Freedom of association is one of the liberties explicitly protected by the Fifth Amendment.

   (C) The right to freedom of association is explicitly articulated in the First Amendment, along with the rights of speech, press, assembly, and religion.

   (D) The right to freedom of association is explicitly articulated in the Ninth Amendment.

8.2.   In *NAACP v. Alabama*, 357 U.S. 449 (1958), the State of Alabama sought to force the NAACP to produce records and papers showing the names and addresses of its Alabama members and agents. The NAACP objected to the disclosure claiming that its members might suffer retaliation. In the *NAACP* case, the Court held that:

   (A) The fact that any harm the NAACP's members might face from disclosure of their membership would come from private action and not the state meant that the risk of such harm did not enter into the First Amendment analysis.

   (B) The NAACP's right to freedom of association protected it from being required to disclose its membership lists.

   (C) The right to freedom of association does not apply to membership lists.

   (D) The right to freedom of association does not apply to corporations and entities like the NAACP.

8.3.   In *West Virginia State Board of Education v. Barnette*, 319 U.S. 624 (1943), the state adopted a resolution ordering that the salute to the flag become "a regular part of the program of activities in the public schools, that all teachers and pupils shall be required to participate in the salute honoring the Nation represented by the Flag; provided, however, that refusal to salute the Flag be regarded as an Act of insubordination, and shall be dealt with accordingly." Please summarize the holding in *Barnette*.

ANSWER:

8.4.   In *Hurley v. Irish-American Gay, Lesbian and Bisexual Group of Boston*, 515 U.S. 557 (1995), a group representing Irish-American gays, lesbians, and bisexuals, called GLIB, sought inclusion in Boston's annual St. Patrick's Day parade. The parade was run by a private group that objected to GLIB's message, and the group excluded GLIB from the parade. GLIB sued, alleging a violation of Massachusetts's law banning sexual orientation discrimination in places of public accommodation. In *Hurley*, the Court held that:

(A)   GLIB had a free speech right to participate in the St. Patrick's Day parade.

(B)   The private group that organized the parade had a First Amendment right to exclude GLIB.

(C)   The right to freedom of association does not extend to parades.

(D)   GLIB did not have a free speech right to march in the parade, but it had a right to do so under the Massachusetts law, and that right ultimately prevailed.

8.5.   In *Boy Scouts of America v. Dale*, 530 U.S. 640 (2000), the Boy Scouts asserted that homosexual conduct was inconsistent with the values it seeks to instill. For that reason it revoked the adult membership of Dale, a former Eagle Scout, when the Scouts learned that he had publicly come out as gay and was, in the Court's description, "a gay rights activist." Dale sued, claiming a violation of New Jersey's public accommodations law that outlawed sexual discrimination in public accommodations. In *Dale*, the Court held that:

(A)   The New Jersey public accommodations law trumps the Boy Scouts' right to freedom of association.

(B)   Dale had a right under the New Jersey law to participate in the Boy Scouts, and vindication of that right did not violate the Scouts' First Amendment rights.

(C)   The Boy Scouts' claim of freedom of association prevailed over Dale's claim based on New Jersey's public accommodations law.

(D)   Discrimination against gays and lesbians is impermissible under the Constitution.

8.6.   *Board of Regents of the University of Wisconsin System v. Southworth*, 529 U.S. 217 (2000), involved an annual University of Wisconsin student activity fee. The fund created by this fee was used to support student organizations. Funding was provided on a viewpoint-neutral basis. Students sued, challenging the activity fee to the extent that it required them to contribute to the speech activities of organizations with which they disagreed. Which of the following statements was **not** a part of the Court's analysis in *Southworth*?

(A) Students could make a First Amendment claim despite the fact that their attendance at the university was completely voluntary.

(B) The University must provide some protection to its students' First Amendment interests.

(C) Students are entitled to protections designed to ensure that the program is administered in a viewpoint-neutral manner.

(D) Student activity fees are not subject to First Amendment protections.

PART II
THE RELIGION CLAUSES

9.1. By its explicit terms, the Establishment Clause of the United States Constitution applies:

(A) To all governments (federal, state, and local).

(B) To the states only.

(C) To the entire federal government, but only to the federal government.

(D) Only to Congress.

9.2. As interpreted and applied by the courts today, the Establishment Clause of the United States Constitution applies:

(A) To all governments (federal, state, and local).

(B) To the states only.

(C) To the entire federal government, but only to the federal government.

(D) To Congress only.

9.3. Which of the following statements best reflects the scope of the Establishment Clause?

(A) The Establishment Clause has only been applied when the government has attempted to declare an "official" religion.

(B) The Establishment Clause has only been applied when the government has tried to mandate church attendance.

(C) The Establishment Clause has only been applied to situations when the government has tried to declare an official religion, mandate attendance at church, or require individuals to profess a belief or disbelief in a particular religion.

(D) The Establishment Clause has been interpreted as applying to a variety of governmental actions beyond just the establishment of an "official" religion.

9.4. To which of the following activities has the Establishment Clause **not** been applied?

(A) Private (individual) prayer in public settings.

(B) Government-provided financial aid to religious organizations.

(C) Official prayer in public schools.

(D) Government-sponsored Christmas displays.

9.5. Every December, the City of Indian Creek erects a Christian nativity scene in front of City Hall. A local group challenges the city's action, claiming that it amounts to an unconstitutional establishment of religion. Which of the following statements most accurately reflects how a court would decide that claim?

(A) If the nativity scene is accompanied by other symbols representing Christmas, such as a secular display of boxes wrapped like Christmas gifts, the court would probably uphold the nativity scene.

(B) Because the nativity scene unquestionably conveys a religious message, a court would probably strike it down.

(C) The nativity scene would be constitutional regardless of the context in which it appeared, given government's right to acknowledge the religious beliefs of the citizenry.

(D) Because the government did not compel any worship of any sort, the nativity scene would be constitutional.

9.6. Which of the following statements accurately states the general rule for the Establishment Clause?

(A) The Establishment Clause does not focus on the effect a government action may have with regard to promoting religion, but concerns itself solely with the purpose behind the government action.

(B) The Establishment Clause is violated if a government action does not have a legitimate secular purpose.

(C) If the government action has a legitimate secular purpose and the principal effect of that action is not to advance religion, then the government action is constitutional.

(D) The Court does not examine whether a government action creates an excessive entanglement between religion and government, due to the sensitive nature of that inquiry, which would require the Court to examine how a government's action affects religious authorities.

9.7. The State of Madison opens every legislative session with a prayer from a clergyman, picked from a rotating list of clergy representing all major denominations. What is the current law regarding such legislative prayers?

(A) Such prayers are constitutional; since the original Constitution called for the opening of congressional sessions with a prayer, it is clear the drafters of the First Amendment intended such a practice to continue.

(B) Such prayers are constitutional, given the long history of the opening of legislative sessions with prayers.

(C) Such prayers are constitutional as long as all denominations get an equal chance to provide a chaplain.

(D) Such prayers are unconstitutional.

9.8. The State of Jackson provides that property used "exclusively for religious, educational, or charitable purposes" is exempt from property taxes. Is this tax exemption constitutional?

(A) YES, because tax law is not subject to the Establishment Clause, given the unique characteristics of a state's taxing function.

(B) YES, because tax breaks for religious organizations, even if not combined with similar tax breaks for education or charitable properties, are a permissible accommodation of religion.

(C) YES, because the Jackson law promotes a legitimate secular purpose of assisting nonprofit institutions thought to benefit the community.

(D) NO, because any assistance to religion violates the Establishment Clause.

9.9. Which of the following statements *inaccurately* states the Supreme Court's approach to government vouchers that students can use to pay for tuition in parochial schools?

(A) The Court considers whether the aid goes directly to the schools or flows through the student and his/her parents through their choice of where the student attends school.

(B) The Court considers whether the aid could have been used at non-parochical private schools.

(C) The Court expresses great concern when most voucher money ends up being used at parochial schools.

(D) The Court does not express particular concern when the amount of voucher aid is closely tied to the cost of tuition at religious schools, but is under the cost of most private non-religious schools.

9.10. The State of Wilson faces a crisis in educating its poorest students, who are failing in the state's public schools. To combat the problem, Wilson enacts a voucher program, whereby the state's poorest students are given vouchers that they can use either at traditional public schools, alternative public schools, or private schools. Most students elect to stay in traditional public schools, where the vouchers allow purchase of extra tutoring sessions. However, of the students who elect some other approach, the vast majority enrolls in Catholic private schools, since there are very few alternative public schools, and private but secular private schools charge higher tuition than Catholic schools, which are subsidized by their parishes. Indeed, the value of the vouchers is essentially equal to the average cost of tuition at a Catholic school. In order to allay fears that state money will be used to spread religious intolerance, the plan provides that "no voucher money may be used for schools where religious intolerance is preached." Is this program constitutional?

ANSWER:

9.11. In response to pressure from parents, the School Board of Jackson City requires that, whenever the theory of evolution is taught in science class, equal mention is made of the theory of creation from the Book of Genesis. The Board's resolution notes that its aim is "simply to provide equal time to secular and religious explanations of the appearance of human life." Is the resolution constitutional?

ANSWER:

9.12. The School Board of Jackson City enacts an ordinance requiring that a local member of the clergy give a generic religious blessing at the start of the elementary school commencement exercise program. Children are not required to attend the ceremony, but most do, as it is generally seen as a major milestone. Clergy are chosen from a list, rotating between members of different religions represented in Jackson City. Is the ordinance constitutional?

ANSWER:

9.13. The State of Adams enacts a law reimbursing parents for private school tuition, in order to counteract the high cost of private education and to maintain a diversity of educational options for parents. Approximately 85% of the private schools in Adams are run by the Catholic or the Baptist Churches. There is no requirement that parents send their children to a religious school in order to get the reimbursement. Is the law constitutional?

ANSWER:

9.14. The State of Jefferson's constitution forbids use of state funds for religious education. Jefferson has a plan called "Jefferson Hope Scholarships" (JHS) that provides high-scoring high school students in Jefferson with money that can be used for tuition at any college in Jefferson. Consistent with the state's constitution, which includes a strong separation of church and state provision, the JHS program forbids providing money for students seeking religious education, which is defined as "pursuing a course of study devoted to religion." Thus, JHS recipients can attend religious schools and take religious courses, but they cannot major in religious studies. James Jameson, a JHS recipient, declares his intention to enroll in missionary studies at a Baptist college in Jefferson and is promptly disqualified from participation in the JHS program. Is the state's action constitutional?

ANSWER:

9.15. A Kentucky law prohibits the teaching of evolution in public schools, "to foster an appreciation of the role of a supreme being in mankind's origins." Based on the holding in *Epperson v. Arkansas*, 393 U.S. 97 (1968), it is safe to say that:

(A) The Kentucky law is constitutional because states have inherent jurisdiction over the educational content of their schools.

(B) The Kentucky law is unconstitutional as an establishment of religion.

(C) The Kentucky law is constitutional so long as the state does not mandate the teaching of creationism.

(D) Since the theory of evolution is an essential component of "secular humanism," it cannot be taught in public schools without running afoul of the Establishment Clause.

9.16. Which of the following gives the best description of the Establishment Clause test from *Lemon v. Kurtzman*, 403 U.S. 602 (1971)?

(A) It reflects an approach to the Establishment Clause that allows government to promote religion in general as long as it does not single out any particular religion for especially favorable or unfavorable treatment.

(B) It reflects an approach to the Establishment Clause that looks to governmental intent as the touchstone; as long as the government has no intent to promote religion, the *Lemon* test means that the government action will not violate the Establishment Clause.

(C) It reflects an approach to the Establishment Clause that ignores intent, and focuses simply on whether the government action has the effect of promoting or inhibiting religion.

(D) It reflects an approach to the Establishment Clause that seeks to determine, among other things, whether the challenged action inappropriately entangles government in religious matters.

9.17. The State of New Kent wishes to pay for elementary school instruction in religious schools. In order to avoid government-paid teachers engaging in religious instruction, the New Kent program requires a government inspector to monitor the classes taught by state-paid teachers, to ensure that those teachers do not perform religious instruction. Would this proviso in the New Kent program satisfy the Establishment Clause?

(A) YES, as long as the government was performing the monitoring "very closely."

(B) YES, as long as government was making "a good faith effort" to prevent state-paid teachers from engaging in religious instruction.

(C) NO, because the proviso itself would entangle the government in religion.

(D) NO, because any state aid to a parochial school would violate the Establishment Clause.

9.18. Halford High School has a policy of making its classrooms available to community groups who wish to meet. The Halford City Bible Study Group wishes to reserve a room but is denied, because that group wishes to engage in religious speech. Halford High explains that it must deny that group access in order to avoid running afoul of the Establishment Clause. Is the school correct?

(A) The school has a point that it would be violating the Establishment Clause if it allowed the group to meet in the high school; however, that interest would be outweighed by the countervailing interest in not denying access to one group when the government had created a public forum.

(B) The school has a point that it would be violating the Establishment Clause if it allowed the group to meet in the high school, and that concern would be enough to justify the school's denial of access.

(C) There is no Establishment Clause problem when the school makes its facilities open to all community groups on a non-discriminatory basis, including religious groups.

(D) The school could only allow access to the group if the school monitored the speech that took place during that meeting to ensure that it did not spread a message of religious intolerance.

9.19. In order to expand educational opportunities for students, the federal government enacts a program that provides federal money to institutions, including religious institutions, to build facilities that would not be used for religious instruction. Does such a program violate the Establishment Clause?

(A) YES, because it provides direct aid to religious schools without the intervention of a private decision-maker such as a student or parent.

(B) NO, because expanding educational opportunities by encouraging their construction is a legitimate secular interest that government may seek to promote.

(C) NO, because aid to religious educational institutions, as opposed to churches themselves, is never unconstitutional.

(D) YES, because such aid, by defraying costs of the secular component of the education, would assist in religious instruction by indirectly allowing religious instruction to proceed at a lower cost.

9.20. The federal government, acting under its Commerce Clause and Spending Clause authority, enacts a law requiring that no state burden the religious practices of any person housed in a state institution that receives federal funds unless such a burden is justified by a compelling government interest and is the least restrictive means of achieving that interest. The State of North Utopia receives federal funds for its prisons. When the warden refuses a Buddhist prisoner's request for a worship space the prisoner sues under the federal law. What result?

(A) The prisoner probably loses, because the federal law probably violates the Establishment Clause by protecting religious exercise rights more than other constitutional rights.

(B) The prisoner probably wins because the Establishment Clause does not apply to the states.

(C) The prisoner probably wins because the Establishment Clause does not require that statutory protections for free religious exercise be paired with analogous protections for other rights.

(D) The prisoner probably loses because any protection for religious exercise rights would violate the Establishment Clause.

9.21. Which of the following statements is most accurate?

(A) The Supreme Court has consistently approached Establishment Clause cases from a strict separationist perspective that is inherently skeptical of all government aid to religion.

(B) The Supreme Court has consistently approached Establishment Clause cases from a perspective that allows government encouragement of religion generally, as long as it does not prefer one religion over another.

(C) The Supreme Court has consistently approached Establishment Clause cases from a perspective that seeks to ensure government neutrality between religion and non-religion.

(D)   The Supreme Court has often oscillated between various approaches to Establishment Clause cases, depending on the factual context and the composition of the Court at that time.

9.22.   The commissioners of Miller County, Texas, pass a resolution requiring the posting of plaques of the Ten Commandments on all courthouse walls, "as a recognition of the central role of Christianity in the American legal system." A citizen then sues to have the plaques removed as a violation of the Establishment Clause. In response to the lawsuit, the commissioners pass another resolution, requiring the posting of plaques of the Ten Commandments as well as excerpts from the Declaration of Independence and the Mayflower Compact referencing religion and God. After the citizen renews her lawsuit the commissioners enact a third resolution, requiring the posting of the Commandments and other documents, including the lyrics to the Star Spangled Banner, the Emancipation Proclamation and the Bill of Rights, and explanations of these documents' significance to American history and law. The citizen again renews her suit. What result?

(A)   The County wins: even the original postings would be constitutional since they did not coerce anyone to profess a particular religious belief, so there is no constitutional problem with posting the Commandments along with the more secular documents.

(B)   The County wins: the earlier postings might violate the Establishment Clause but the new ones do not, and the fact that the postings were changed in response to litigation is irrelevant to the constitutional issue.

(C)   The County loses: the earlier postings clearly evince the County's intent with regard to the final, less religion-centered postings. The fact that the County clearly intended to promote a religious message renders even the final postings unconstitutional.

(D)   The County loses: any posting of any picture or document with a potentially religious message would violate the Establishment Clause.

9.23.   The State of New Kent has a sculpture garden on its capitol grounds featuring sculptures recounting the state's history and the groups that make up the state. Forty years ago, the Fraternal Order of Hawks donated a large sculpture of the Ten Commandments to the state, which places it in the sculpture garden. Today, a citizen sues, alleging that the Ten Commandments sculpture violates the Establishment Clause. Which of the following inquiries would be the *least* influential in a court's consideration of this claim?

(A)   Whether the display had a connection to the historical heritage of the state.

(B)   Whether the display had been on the capitol grounds for a long period without anyone complaining about its religious content.

(C) Whether the display was potentially susceptible to a religious interpretation.

(D) Whether the display was part of a grouping of sculptures that spoke to secular themes.

10.1. At the outset, it is worthwhile for us to think about why the Free Exercise Clause was inserted in the United States Constitution. In regard to the motivations of the colonists (more appropriately, the new Americans), which of the following *inaccurately* describes a reason for including that Clause in the Constitution:

(A) Many early immigrants to the American colonies came to the Americas fleeing religious persecution in Europe.

(B) A significant percentage of immigrants to the American colonies came seeking to escape from being taxed to support religions to which they did not belong.

(C) A significant percentage of immigrants to the American colonies came seeking a place where they could freely exercise their beliefs.

(D) Many immigrants to the American colonies came hoping to create a place of tolerance for all religions and all sects.

10.2. In some instances, there is a conflict between a law and an individual's religious beliefs. For example, suppose that a state law requires that all vehicles traveling on state highways display rear reflectors that help alert overtaking drivers to their presence. The Amish, because of their religious beliefs, object to placing reflectors on their horse drawn buggies and wagons. As a result, the Amish have an irreconcilable conflict between their religious beliefs and their obligation to display the reflectors. Which of the following statements correctly suggests how this conflict should be resolved under the Free Exercise Clause?

(A) In every instance when there is a conflict between the obligations of a law and an individual's religious beliefs, the Free Exercise Clause requires that the obligations of state law give way to the religious practice.

(B) An analysis of the history of the Free Exercise Clause suggests that the obligations of a statute have never been forced to give way to a religious concern or practice.

(C) There have been instances when the Free Exercise Clause has trumped the obligations of a statute, and required accommodation of a religious practice.

(D) The Establishment Clause prohibits the states from accommodating a religious belief when there is a conflict with the obligations of a state law.

10.3. Which of the following statements accurately reflects the definition of religion for purposes of the First Amendment?

(A) A religious belief, in order to be credited for Free Exercise purposes, must be consistent with the official dogma of that religion.

(B) The courts will not inquire into whether the individual making a Free Exercise claim has a sincere belief in the doctrine he is espousing.

(C) The Court has consistently embraced a broader definition of "religion" for purposes of the Free Exercise Clause than it has for purposes of the Establishment Clause.

(D) The Court has encountered great difficulty in attempting to define the term "religion."

10.4. Please write a short answer explaining some of the reasons why the Framers might have included the Free Exercise Clause in the First Amendment.

ANSWER:

10.5. One of the things that the Court has struggled to do is to define the concept of religion. In *United States v. Ballard*, 322 U.S. 78 (1944), the defendant was indicted for obtaining money under false pretenses because the government felt that his religious claims were fraudulent. Among other things, he had used aliases such as "Saint Germain, Jesus, George Washington, and Godfre Ray King," and claimed that he had been selected as a "divine messenger" through which the words of the divine would be communicated to mankind under the teachings commonly known as the "I Am" movement. In addition, the defendant claimed that he had the power to heal incurable ailments and diseases, and that he had in fact cured hundreds of afflicted persons. Which of the following statements does *not* reflect the Court's analysis in *Ballard*?

(A) Free Exercise Clause protections apply to more than mainstream religions.

(B) Freedom of thought, which includes freedom of religious belief, is basic in a society of free men.

(C) Courts may not inquire into the objective truth or falsity of a person's religious beliefs.

(D) Ballard could be convicted of fraud because the statements he made about religious matters were false.

10.6. In *Wisconsin v. Yoder*, 406 U.S. 205 (1972), members of the Old Order Amish religion sought to exempt their children from compulsory school attendance laws. The Amish did so on the ground that their "way of life" was religiously based and was inconsistent with compulsory education laws. Please discuss whether this "way of life" is entitled to protection under the Free Exercise Clause.

ANSWER:

10.7. In *Thomas v. Review Board*, 450 U.S. 707 (1981), a Jehovah's Witness was hired to work in a roll foundry. When the roll foundry closed, he was transferred to a department that fabricated turrets for military tanks. He quit his job, asserting that he could not work on weapons without violating the principles of his religion. No other work was available so he was discharged. His request for unemployment compensation benefits was denied even though he testified that contributing to the production of arms violated his religious beliefs. At trial a fellow Jehovah's Witness testified that working on weapons parts was not "unscriptural." In *Thomas*, the Court held that:

(A) A person's claim for benefits based on his religious beliefs should be denied when his co-religionist interprets the commands of their common faith differently.

(B) A person's Free Exercise claim can be denied where the person is unable to articulate his religious belief "with substantial clarity."

(C) Courts generally do not have the competence to determine whether a person is correctly interpreting the beliefs of his religion.

(D) Courts have an obligation to inquire into the accuracy of a person's interpretation of his religion's beliefs.

10.8. *Reynolds v. United States*, 98 U.S. 145 (1878), involved a federal law prohibiting polygamy as applied to a Mormon whose religion required him to engage in that practice. In *Reynolds*, the Court held that:

(A) The Free Exercise Clause exempts the Mormons from the dictates of the federal anti-polygamy law.

(B) The Court distinguished between "belief" and "conduct," and concluded that the government had broad authority to prohibit religious conduct such as polygamy.

(C) Polygamy is not an "essential" aspect of Mormonism and therefore is not protected under the Free Exercise Clause.

(D) The government may not ban a practice like polygamy when many of its practitioners engage in it for religious reasons.

10.9. In *Sherbert v. Verner*, 374 U.S. 398 (1963), a member of the Seventh-Day Adventist Church was discharged by her employer because she would not work on Saturday, the Sabbath Day of her faith. When she was unable to obtain other employment because her faith precluded Saturday work, she filed a claim for unemployment compensation benefits under the state's unemployment compensation act. The agency administering the program found that the employee's restriction upon her availability for Saturday work brought her within the statute's provision disqualifying for benefits insured workers who fail, without good cause, to accept "suitable work when offered. . . ." In *Sherbert*, the Court held that:

(A) The state law imposed the same kind of burden as a fine for worshipping on Saturday.

(B) The Free Exercise Clause does not protect "peripheral" religious beliefs like the claimant's refusal to work on Saturday.

(C) The claimant's refusal to work constituted "conduct" and therefore was not protected by the Free Exercise Clause.

(D) The Free Exercise Clause does not entitle employees to obtain unemployment compensation when religious beliefs preclude them from accepting work that is offered to them.

10.10. Suppose that a state constitution requires declaration of a belief in God as a prerequisite to assuming public office. Discuss whether this constitutional provision violates the Establishment Clause.

ANSWER:

10.11. *Employment Division v. Smith*, 494 U.S. 872 (1990), involved an Oregon law that prohibited the knowing or intentional possession of a "controlled substance" unless the substance has been prescribed by a medical practitioner. Included on the list of "controlled substances" is the drug peyote, a hallucinogen. The plaintiffs were fired from their jobs with a private drug rehabilitation organization because they ingested peyote for sacramental purposes at a ceremony of a Native American church of which both are members. When they applied for unemployment compensation, they were determined to be ineligible because they had been discharged for work-related "misconduct." In *Smith* the Court held that:

(A) The employees' free exercise rights gave them a constitutional right to use peyote and insulated them from being denied unemployment compensation on the basis that they had engaged in misconduct.

(B) The employees were not entitled to protection under the Free Exercise Clause because the law criminalizing use of peyote was supported by a compelling government interest.

(C) The employees were not entitled to protection under the Free Exercise Clause because the state criminal law was a rule of general applicability requiring adherence by all, despite religious objections.

(D) Religious use of peyote is constitutionally protected.

10.12. *Church of the Lukumi Babalu Aye, Inc. v. City of Hialeah*, 508 U.S. 520 (1993), involved a Florida ordinance that prohibited killing animals, but with exceptions that effectively limited its restriction to ritual animal sacrifice. The law was hastily passed in response to news that a small Caribbean-based religion planned to engage in animal sacrifice in the city. The church challenged the ordinance. In *Church of the Lukumi*, the Court held that:

(A) Since the Free Exercise Clause protects only belief, and not conduct, the Santeria's practice of animal sacrifice is entitled to no constitutional protection.

(B) The law violates the Free Exercise Clause if it discriminates against some or all religious beliefs or regulates or prohibits conduct because it is undertaken for religious reasons.

(C) The Free Exercise Clause does not protect animal sacrifice, given the "material adverse effects" of animal sacrifices on the community.

(D) Because the law is crafted as a general law, despite its exceptions, it does not violate the Free Exercise Clause.

10.13. *Lyng v. Northwest Indian Cemetery Protective Association*, 485 U.S. 439 (1988), involved a United States Forest Service (USFS) project designed to build a road on federal land. As part of this project, the USFS was going to build a 6-mile paved segment through the Chimney Rock section of the Six Rivers National Forest. Indian groups objected claiming that the Chimney Rock area has historically been used for religious purposes. They also claimed that the entire area "is significant as an integral and indispensable part of Indian religious conceptualization and practice." Specific sites are used for certain rituals, and "successful use of the [area] is dependent upon and facilitated by certain qualities of the physical environment, the most important of which are privacy, silence, and an undisturbed natural setting." A study concluded that constructing a road along any of the available routes "would cause serious and irreparable damage to the sacred areas which are an integral and necessary part of the belief systems and lifeway of Northwest California Indian peoples." In *Lyng*, the Court held that:

(A) The Free Exercise Clause precluded the USFS from building the road.

(B) The Free Exercise Clause did not prevent the government from building the road, since government could not operate if it were required to satisfy every citizen's religious needs and desires.

(C) The Indians' claims were not "central" to their religion.

(D) The Free Exercise Clause absolutely protects Indian burial grounds.

10.14. In *Board of Education of Kiryas Joel Village School District v. Grumet*, 512 U.S. 687 (1994), the State of New York authorized the creation of an independent school district in the Village of Kiryas Joel, a village populated almost entirely by Satmar Hasidic Jews, a small sect within Judaism. In the *Kiryas Joel* case, the Court held that:

(A) The district was constitutional because the State of New York was entitled to accommodate the religious beliefs of the Satmar Hasidic Jews in this way.

(B) The district was constitutional because it was permissible for the State of New York to grant a religious preference to a persecuted group like the Satmar Hasidic Jews.

(C) Establishment of the special school district constituted an unconstitutional establishment of religion.

(D) The Establishment Clause does not apply to the creation of special school districts, which is a fundamentally secular task.

10.15. In *Rosenberger v. Rector and Visitors of the University of Virginia*, 515 U.S. 819 (1995), the University of Virginia's Student Activities Fund denied funding to an avowedly religious student publication on the basis that the funding would constitute an establishment of religion. In *Rosenberger*, the Court held that:

(A) The funding denial was permissible because it was justified by the University's legitimate interest in avoiding an establishment of religion.

(B) The funding denial constituted an unconstitutional discrimination against speech based on its viewpoint.

(C) The funding denial was constitutional because the Student Activities Fund was financed out of student fees, and the funding would have constituted an unconstitutional exaction in support of religion.

(D) The Establishment Clause does not apply to student activity fund decisions.

10.16. A member of the Old Order Amish refuses to pay Social Security taxes on the ground that he objects to receiving public insurance benefits and paying taxes to support public insurance funds. Please discuss whether the tax objector can be forced to pay the taxes.

ANSWER:

10.17. In *Jimmy Swaggart Ministries v. Board of Equalization*, 493 U.S. 378 (1990), a religious group refused to pay sales and use taxes on religious literature. Although the tax applied to the sale of all goods and services, the group claimed that it could not be applied to the sale of religious literature. In *Jimmy Swaggart*, the Court held that:

(A) The tax is unconstitutional as applied to religious literature.

(B) The tax is constitutional, even as applied to religious literature, because it is a neutral tax applicable to all goods and services.

(C) The tax is constitutional because state and local governments have an absolute right to tax.

(D) Religious groups cannot object to taxation.

10.18. A state statute requires slow-moving vehicles to display a fluorescent orange-red triangular emblem while operating on state highways. The requirement was enacted for safety purposes. The Old Order Amish, who often drive horse-drawn buggies on public highways, object to this requirement because it violates their religious belief against displaying "loud colors" and "worldly symbols." The Amish are willing to line the outside of their buggies with silver reflective tape and to adorn the buggies with lighted red lanterns. The state deems these actions insufficient. Please discuss whether the Amish are entitled to an exemption from the requirement.

ANSWER:

10.19. In *Cantwell v. Connecticut*, 310 U.S. 296 (1940), Cantwell and his two sons, Jehovah's Witnesses and ordained ministers, were arrested and convicted of attempting to sell religious magazines without a permit and of disorderly conduct. In *Cantwell*, in response to Cantwell's free exercise claims, the Court held that:

(A) The right to freely exercise religion applies only to the right to attend the religious services of one's choice.

(B) The statute prohibiting solicitation before getting a license violated Cantwell's right to free exercise, given the degree of discretion the town had to deny or grant the license.

(C) The Cantwells were protected, if at all, only under the freedom of speech provisions of the First Amendment.

(D) The Establishment Clause precludes the government from regulating the distribution of religious literature.

10.20. In *Goldman v. Weinberger*, 475 U.S. 503 (1986), a Jewish soldier claimed that the

Free Exercise Clause allowed him to wear a yarmulke in conjunction with his military uniform, despite an Air Force regulation mandating uniform dress. In *Goldman* the Court held that:

(A) The prohibition should be upheld because of the special nature of the military, which justifies infringements on individual rights that might not be acceptable in civilian society.

(B) The prohibition constitutes an invalid infringement of Goldman's right to freely exercise his religion.

(C) The prohibition on wearing the yarmulke constituted an establishment of Christianity, in violation of the Establishment Clause.

(D) The Free Exercise Clause protects all religious symbols.

10.21. In *O'Lone v. Shabazz*, 482 U.S. 342 (1987), respondents were Muslim prisoners who challenged policies adopted by prison officials. Under the policies, prisoners who were to be transferred from maximum security to minimum security prisons were first assigned to work gangs that labored outside the prison. Because these transitional prisoners were outside the building, they were unable to attend Jumu'ah, a weekly Muslim congregational service regularly held in the main prison building and in a separate facility known as "the Farm." Jumu'ah is commanded by the Koran and must be held every Friday after the sun reaches its zenith and before the Asr, or afternoon prayer. Prison officials refused to allow "gang" workers to return to "the Farm" during the day because of security risks and administrative problems. As a result, those assigned to gangs were forced to miss Jumu'ah. Muslim prisoners sued seeking an accommodation. In *O'Lone* the Court held that:

(A) Prisoners have an absolute right to freely exercise their religion even in prison.

(B) The prison regulations would survive only if they were narrowly tailored to meet a compelling government interest.

(C) Evaluation of penalogical objectives is committed to the considered judgment of prison administrators.

(D) The Free Exercise Clause does not apply in the prison context, as free religious exercise is one of the rights prisoners give up.

FINAL EXAM QUESTIONS

1. In *New York Times Co. v. Sullivan*, 376 U.S. 254 (1964), the Court held that the actual malice standard should apply to:

    (A) Political speech.

    (B) Only unpaid political speech.

    (C) Speech relating to public officials.

    (D) Speech relating to both public figures and private individuals.

2. When the Court refers to "public figures," it sometimes refers to "vortex" public figures. Please write a short answer describing the concept of a "vortex" public figure.

    ANSWER:

3. In *Hustler Magazine v. Falwell*, 485 U.S. 46 (1988), the Court held that:

    (A) "Outrageous" parodies are not entitled to constitutional protection.

    (B) Even outrageous parodies deserve constitutional protection.

    (C) Parodies are entitled to constitutional protection only if they are "fair."

    (D) Parodies have nothing to do with free speech.

4. A bookstore in Columbia City, in the State of Columbia, wishes to sell a book entitled "Dirty Deeds in Denver." As the name implies, the book describes and shows pictures of sexual acts, situated in various landmarks around the City of Denver. Each chapter of the book begins with a very short description of the landmark before getting to the portrayals and pictures of sexual activity. The District Attorney of Columbia City seeks to have the book banned. Can the book be banned?

    (A) The book cannot be banned because any speech dealing with sexual expression is protected just like speech dealing with any other type of activity.

    (B) The book cannot be banned because the descriptions of Denver provide the book with "the modicum of literary or other merit" that the Supreme Court has held makes a work non-obscene and thus constitutionally protected.

(C) The book can possibly be banned because the descriptions of Denver probably don't rise to the level of "serious literary, artistic, political, or scientific value" that the Supreme Court has held makes a work non-obscene and thus constitutionally protected.

(D) As long as a jury in Denver finds the book to appeal primarily to the prurient interest, rather than any legitimate interest in Denver, the book can be banned.

5. A state statute bans not only the possession of child pornography, but also the possession of "virtual child pornography," that is, computer images that might have been created solely on a computer or based on a photograph of a live child model. How should a reviewing court rule on the statute?

(A) Because it is difficult to know whether virtual child pornography actually used live models, the court would allow the legislature to prohibit its possession, given the need to protect children.

(B) Because it is difficult to know whether virtual child pornography actually used live models, the court would probably err on the side of free speech and strike the restriction down.

(C) The harm of child pornography lies in the appetites it feeds for abusing children; thus, the court would have no difficulty upholding the restriction, regardless of whether or not live models were used.

(D) As long as child pornography of any sort qualifies as non-obscene under the *Miller v. California* test for obscenity, it is constitutionally protected.

6. In order to prevent beer sellers from engaging in "price wars" that reduce the price of beer and thus increase consumption, the State of Franklin imposes a ban on the advertising of beer prices. The State defends the ban by pointing to the dangers of excessive alcohol consumption. Is the restriction valid?

(A) YES. Under the 21st Amendment, states have significant leeway to regulate alcohol, which would include this type of restriction.

(B) YES. Without even considering the 21st Amendment, states have broad power to regulate commercial activity. Because Franklin could have restricted beer sales or regulated the price of beer, it could take the lesser step of restricting speech about the price.

(C) NO. Because the state could have regulated the price or availability of beer, it did not need to restrict speech about the price of beer in order to satisfy its goal of restricting alcohol use.

(D) NO. Because commercial speech gets full First Amendment protection, any content-based restriction on speech, such as this one, would be subject to strict scrutiny and probably wouldn't survive.

7.   Would a court uphold or strike down a statute that required all schoolchildren to stand and recite the Pledge of Allegiance every morning in the classroom?

   (A) The court would probably uphold it, given the government's compelling interest in fostering a sense of patriotism.

   (B) The court would probably uphold it since nobody would be actually prevented from speaking.

   (C) The court would probably strike it down because government may not coerce speech, just as it may not restrict it.

   (D) The court would probably strike it down because the government has no legitimate interest in encouraging patriotism or any other particular political viewpoint.

Questions 8 and 9 relate to the following fact pattern:

After a hotly contested local election in which charges of electoral fraud are made, Mandy Martyr leads a protest rally to the steps of City Council. After making an impassioned speech (which has at its theme the constant refrain, "The doors of government have been closed! We must open them again!"), she ceremoniously takes her voter registration card out and burns it to protest the alleged electoral fraud which she claims occurred. That action plus her speech energizes the crowd to start chanting, "Let us in!" After five minutes of such chanting, a protester breaks down the door of City Hall and the protesters rush in, destroying a large amount of city property.

8.   Mandy is charged with inciting a riot. Please discuss whether she has a First Amendment defense to that charge.

ANSWER:

9.   Mandy is charged with destruction of her voter card (which you can assume is illegal under state law). Please discuss whether she has a First Amendment defense to that charge.

ANSWER:

10.   Robert Renfro, a law student, attends a session of municipal court one day with a jacket on the back of which he has sewn the words "Screw the Police." The bailiff asks Renfro to remove the jacket; when he refuses, the bailiff arrests him for disturbing the peace. Which of the following, if true, would provide the strongest support for upholding the conviction?

   (A) It was established at trial that a number of spectators were in the courtroom.

(B)   Renfro had gotten the bailiff's attention and then turned the back of the jacket so the bailiff could see it, as a taunt.

(C)   A jury had determined that the words on Renfro's jacket would be offensive to a reasonable person in the community.

(D)   All of these facts, if true, would provide equal support for upholding the conviction.

11.   Mac Malicious procures a magazine entitled Young Ones, which contains stories of pre-teen sex and pictures of pre-teen girls and boys engaged in a variety of sexual positions, alone and with each other. After it is discovered that he possesses such material in his home, he is arrested and charged with possession of child pornography. Mac asserts a First Amendment defense. Will Mac win or lose?

(A)   Mac loses unless he can demonstrate that the material satisfies the *Miller v. California* standard of having serious literary, artistic, political, or scientific value.

(B)   Mac loses because the material is unprotected under the First Amendment.

(C)   Mac wins because he possessed the material in his own home.

(D)   Mac loses because pornography with models of any age is unprotected by the Constitution and may be prohibited if a state chooses to do so.

12.   The City of Watertown decides that there are too many news racks on its sidewalks, causing visual blight and litter. It enacts an ordinance prohibiting the further placement of "commercial handbill" racks on public sidewalks. The ordinance defines "commercial handbills" explicitly to exclude daily newspapers and to include "any circular published for the primary purpose of advertising a good or a service." Is the ordinance constitutional?

ANSWER:

13.   High school students wear armbands to school to indicate their opposition to an increasingly unpopular war, despite the principal's warning against such conduct. The students are suspended and challenge that suspension, claiming their First Amendment rights were violated. What is the likely approach the court would take in considering their claim?

(A)   The court would probably rule in the school's favor, noting that schools in their supervisory capacity have near-complete control over the conduct of students while on campus.

(B) The court would probably rule in the students' favor, as long as there was no indication to the court that the wearing of the armbands was likely to cause significant disciplinary problems.

(C) The court would probably rule in the school's favor, noting that the wearing of clothing is conduct and not speech, and thus it is outside the protection of the First Amendment.

(D) The court would probably rule in the students' favor, since such conduct would surely be protected for adults.

14. In order to protect children from indecent content on the Internet, Congress enacts a statute that prohibits the dissemination of any information deemed inappropriate for children where children may access it. The statute further states that individuals may post such materials on the Internet, free of legal liability, if they require a credit card number to access the material. Is the statute constitutional?

(A) NO, because it prohibits too much speech.

(B) YES, because it aims at the protection of children.

(C) NO, because speech on the Internet enjoys absolute protection.

(D) YES, because the Internet is non-governmental property, where more lenient speech restriction rules apply.

15. Are there differences between the rights corporations enjoy to spend money to express political views, depending on whether the corporation is a for-profit corporation formed to earn money or a non-for-profit corporation formed to express political opinions?

(A) NO, there are no differences, due to the impossibility of determining which corporations are formed for which purposes.

(B) NO, there are no differences, since direct expenditures are equally protected for all.

(C) YES, there are differences: for-profit corporations can be more heavily regulated with regard to their ability to make direct expenditures.

(D) YES, there is a difference, but it turns not on the nature of the corporation, but of the speech. In particular, politically-motivated campaign contributions are more protected than contributions motivated by a mere desire to advance a corporation's own private interests.

16. Upon election as sheriff in Adams County, Smith, a Democrat, fires all the non-civil service Republicans in the office and replaces them with Democrats. To what extent can the sheriff do this, consistent with the First Amendment?

(A) The sheriff has significant latitude to make these personnel changes, since political patronage has a long history in the United States.

(B) The sheriff has significant latitude to make these personnel changes based on party affiliation on the theory that subordinates of the same political persuasion will work more effectively together.

(C) The sheriff probably cannot do this, due to the First Amendment interests of the employees.

(D) The First Amendment has nothing to say about this issue, since belonging to a political party is not protected by the First Amendment.

17. Fort Flix, a military installation, maintains streets and roads; these streets are open to the public but the base commander has the authority to close them to civilian traffic if he deems it necessary. A candidate for political office seeks to stand on one of these streets and distribute leaflets in favor of his campaign. When the candidate is denied his request, with the commander citing a rule against political activity on base, the candidate sues, claiming his First Amendment rights have been violated. Should the candidate win or lose?

(A) The candidate probably loses.

(B) The candidate loses unless he can show that the base granted permission for religious, charity, and musical groups to appear and speak on the base.

(C) The candidate wins regardless of whether the base granted permission for religious, charity, and musical groups to appear and speak on the base.

(D) The candidate probably loses, even if other candidates in that election were allowed to speak on the base.

18. Which of the following criteria has **not** been cited by the Court as a factor in determining whether a particular piece of government-owned property is a public forum?

(A) The tradition of the availability of that location for speech.

(B) The extent to which speech is compatible with the usual functioning of the property.

(C) Whether the primary purpose of the place is for speech.

(D) Whether more speech could be expected if the area was denominated a public forum.

19. The State of Adams enacts a law making it a crime to discriminate against women in the workplace. Subsequent interpretation of that statute establishes that discrimination includes harassment, such as inappropriate jokes and

propositions. Timmy Burger, a fast food outlet, is fined by the state because one of its male employees made an off-color joke to a female employee that a court found to constitute harassment. If Timmy Burger can assert the speech rights of the male employee, and if the joke was indeed harassment, what would be the result if Timmy Burger alleged that the First Amendment protected that speech?

(A) The Court might well **accept** the argument: a rule against sexual harassment speech is a content-based restriction on speech since it prohibits sexual harassment but not other types of harassment (e.g., harassment based on sexual orientation); thus, the court would subject it to strict scrutiny.

(B) The Court would probably **reject** the argument, as the Supreme Court has stated that bans on sexual harassment speech are akin to secondary effects regulation, since they are aimed at a substantive wrong rather than at expression *per se*.

(C) The Court would **reject** the argument since harassment is akin to fighting words, which are unprotected.

(D) The Court would **accept** the argument because harassing speech is protected by the Constitution.

20. The town of Quiet Haven is roiled by a series of cross-burnings on the property of black residents. In response, the town council enacts the following ordinance: "Whosoever commits an act, including but not limited to, the burning of a cross, which the perpetrator has reason to believe will cause resentment, anger, fear or anguish on the basis of the victim's race, shall be guilty of a misdeameanor. This ordinance shall only apply to conduct which constitutes unprotected 'fighting words' as that term is understood under the United States Constitution." The next time a cross-burning occurs, the police arrest a local man and charge him with violating the ordinance. Please discuss whether the conviction should stand.

ANSWER:

21. In *Freedman v. Maryland*, 380 U.S. 51 (1965), the Court dealt with a licensing scheme that applied to motion pictures. In the trial court, the defendant was convicted of failing to seek a license by submitting a film to the licensor. In *Freedman*, the Court held that:

(A) Licensing schemes for films always constitute unconstitutional prior restraints.

(B) Prior restraints on distribution of all art and ideas (including movies) are unconstitutional in all circumstances.

(C) The licensing scheme lacked sufficient safeguards for confining the censor's action to judicially-determined constitutional limits, and therefore contains the same vice as a statute delegating excessive administrative discretion.

(D)   Movies are not entitled to First Amendment protection.

22.   In a number of cases, criminal defendants are faced with extensive and potentially prejudicial pretrial publicity. In some countries, courts impose extensive publishing restrictions on the media to protect against such publicity. In the United States, suppose that a trial court decides to enter a gag order prohibiting all pretrial publicity relating to a pending criminal case. The order would be:

(A)   Probably constitutional because the press does not have a constitutional right to cover events when that coverage would impair a constitutional right, such as the right to a fair trial.

(B)   Probably constitutional because, in the conflict of constitutional values, due process trumps free speech.

(C)   Probably unconstitutional because gag orders of this sort usually violate the First Amendment.

(D)   Probably unconstitutional because the public scrutiny caused by press coverage always redounds to the benefit of the fairness of the trial.

23.   In *Roberts v. United States Jaycees*, 468 U.S. 609 (1984), the Jaycees challenged a Minnesota law that prohibits the organization from discriminating on the basis of sex. Which of the following statements does ***not*** reflect the Court's analysis of whether the Jaycees have a First Amendment right of association to exclude women as members?

(A)   The right of freedom of association extends to highly personal and intimate relationships.

(B)   An assertion by the organization that its associational rights would be impaired by forced inclusion of a particular type of member is not by itself sufficient to uphold that right; further investigation by a court is necessary.

(C)   The membership selectivity of the organization doing the discriminating is relevant to the freedom of association issue.

(D)   Organizations that take positions on public issues have an absolute right to control their membership.

24.   The State of Lincoln imposes a law requiring that all non-essential businesses close on Sundays. The statute states that the law is necessary because people are working too much and not spending enough time with their families. The statute further states that Sundays historically have been viewed as a rest day, and that making any other day of the week a holiday would create a great deal of hardship and confusion. A religious group for whom Wednesday is the holiest day of the week sues, alleging that the statute amounts to an establishment of religion. Does the statute violate the

Establishment Clause?

ANSWER:

25. The School District of Rose City enacts a plan to reimburse the bus fare of elementary students taking the bus to and from school. The plan is open to any elementary student, regardless of whether the student attends public, private, or religious school. Is this aid to religious school students a violation of the Establishment Clause?

ANSWER:

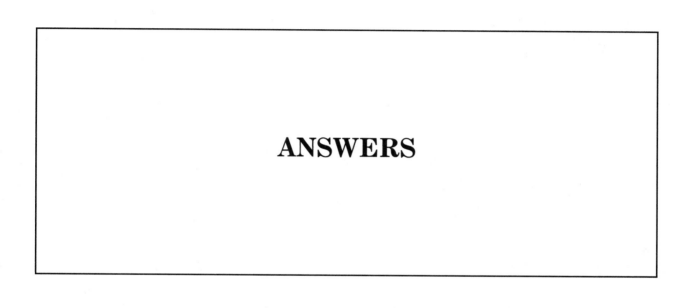

ANSWERS

1.1.   **Answer (B) is correct.** The position that First Amendment rights are not absolute, but instead are subject to balancing and restrictions, has prevailed over Justice Black's position. Justice Holmes' famous statement that "[t]he most stringent protection of free speech would not protect a man in falsely shouting fire in a theatre and causing a panic." *Schenck v. United States*, 249 U.S. 47 (1919), suggests the need for balancing.

Answer (A) is incorrect because it states that the First Amendment should be interpreted literally and absolutely to preclude Congress from exercising any control over speech or the press, is incorrect. This position was articulated by Justice Black in *Konigsberg v. State Bar of California*, 366 U.S. 36, 60–61 (1961), but has since been rejected by the Court. *See Schenck v. United States, infra.*

Answer (C) is incorrect because the statement that First Amendment rights can be abridged only when a "compelling governmental interest" exists is incorrect. Although the Court requires such an interest in some situations, this requirement is not applied in every case. *See Schenck v. United States, infra.*

Answer (D) is incorrect because the statement that First Amendment rights can be abridged whenever a substantial government interest exists is not universally, or even usually, correct. *See Konigsberg v. State Bar of California, supra.*

1.2.   **Answer (A) is correct.** There is little direct evidence regarding the Framers' intent in reference to the First Amendment. *See* RUSSELL L. WEAVER & ARTHUR HELLMAN, THE FIRST AMENDMENT: CASES, MATERIALS & PROBLEMS (LexisNexis 2004).

Answer (B) is incorrect because it suggests that the Framers' intent was recorded in relative detail, and that was not the case. *Id.*

Answer (C) is incorrect because the First Amendment was proposed by the first Congress rather than at the Constitutional Convention. *Id.*

Answer (D) is incorrect because it states that no records were kept at the Constitutional Convention and records were in fact kept. *Id.*

1.3.   **Answer (D) is correct** because any such tradition, if it existed in 1791, was not centuries-old. Libel law continues to threaten speech on public matters in England even today, and the war on taxes on knowledge (in the form of taxes on the press) was still being fought less than a century before 1791. *See Grosjean v. American Press*, 297 U.S. 233 (1936). If anything, the Framers were interested in preserving speech freedoms that were relatively newly-won in England in 1791.

Answer (A) is incorrect because the colonists must have been aware of Crown attempts to repress speech through seditious libel prosecutions during the colonial period. *See* Zechariah Chafee, Free Speech in the United States (1941).

Answer (B) is incorrect because the colonists might have been aware of licensing restrictions. *Id.*

Answer (C) is incorrect because there was, in fact, a widespread perception regarding the need to protect freedom of speech. *Id.*

1.4. **Answer (B) is the statement that was not true.** Under the crime of seditious libel, governments could punish not only false criticisms of government, but also truthful criticisms. In other words, truth was not a defense.

Answer (A) is a correct statement. The crime of seditious libel did provide criminal punishment for those who criticized governmental officials.

Answer (C) is a correct statement. At one point in history, the crime punished not only those who criticized governmental officials, but also those who criticized the clergy.

Answer (D) is a correct statement. Among the punishments that could be imposed for seditious libel was the penalty of imprisonment.

1.5. **Answer (D) is correct** because there is no such theory. *See* Thomas I. Emerson, *Toward a General Theory of the First Amendment*, 72 Yale L.J. 877 (1963).

Answer (A) is incorrect because the "marketplace of ideas" theory (which suggests that all ideas should be allowed into the "marketplace of ideas" and that, in the competition of ideas, the best ideas will emerge) has been advanced for the special status accorded to speech under the First Amendment. *Id.*

Answer (B) is incorrect because most commentators recognize that freedom of speech is essential to the proper functioning of a democratic system of government. *Id.*

Answer (C) is incorrect because individual "self-fulfillment" (which suggests that people should be allowed to speak and receive ideas freely as a necessary aspect of "self-fulfillment") has been advanced as a justification for protecting speech. *Id.*

1.6. **Answer (B) is correct** because it articulates the "safety valve" theory (the idea that, if people are allowed to freely say what they think, they are more likely to "let off steam" in healthy ways rather than by engaging in violence), which is a recognized theory of free speech. *See* Thomas I. Emerson, *Toward a General Theory of the First Amendment*, 72 Yale L.J. 877 (1963).

Answer (A) is incorrect because the "anything goes" theory has never received general acceptance. *Id.*

Answer (C) is incorrect because there is no such theory. *Id.*

Answer (D) is incorrect because there is no such theory. *Id.*

1.7. The "safety valve" theory suggests that speech is accorded special status because it serves as a safety valve for societal pressures. *See* Thomas I. Emerson, *Toward a*

General Theory of the First Amendment, 72 YALE L.J. 877 (1963). The idea is that, if the citizenry is not allowed to express its objections or concerns through speech, it is more likely to do so in less socially acceptable ways (e.g., violence). *Id.* In other words, by allowing people to say what they think, free speech serves as a pressure release that helps to dampen violence. *Id.*

1.8. **Answer (D) is correct.** If certain ideas prevail in the marketplace, they prevail only in the form of public opinion or at the ballot box (in that the citizenry can vote or support the ideas or people that they prefer).

Answer (A) is incorrect. Even though the "marketplace of ideas" metaphor suggests that ideas have economic value, and are bartered and sold like other commodities, the marketplace of ideas theory does not actually involve economic transactions. Ideas are not sold in an economic sense, but are "exchanged" in the rough and tumble of discussion.

Answer (B) is incorrect. The marketplace of ideas theory does not assume that legislation is "bought and sold" via compromises and deals. This is a theory of legislation, but it's not expressed by the marketplace theory.

Answer (C) is incorrect. Even though the marketplace of ideas theory assumes that there will be a competition of ideas, it does not result in a governmental declaration that certain ideas have prevailed. In some instances, ideas will prevail and will prompt governmental action (*e.g.*, opposition to a war may prompt the government to end the war), but it is not generally government's place to declare which ideas are "correct" or "incorrect."

1.9. Although competition in the "marketplace of ideas" can lead to truth, and to the triumph of the best ideas, that is not necessarily so. *See* C. Edwin Baker, *Scope of the First Amendment Freedom of Speech*, 25 U.C.L.A. L. REV. 964 (1978). Indeed, many commentators have concluded that the notion that speech necessarily leads to the discovery of "truth" is "implausible." *Id.* Nevertheless, the theory survives, in part, because there is societal consensus that, in a free society involving democratic principles of government, virtually any idea should be allowed into the "marketplace of ideas." *Id.* A fundamental aspect of a free society is that people should be free to try to persuade others to the correctness of their views, and to try to encourage legislators to adopt a particular course of action. *Id.*

1.10. **Answer (C) is the incorrect answer.** Under the democratic process theory, speech is always protected (not just at the time of elections).

Answer (A) is a correct statement. It is correct to state that, in a democracy, truth flows not from the government to the people, but from the people to the government. That concept is the essence of democracy and reflects a direct repudiation of seditious libel (which made it a crime to criticize the government).

Answer (B) is a correct statement. In a democracy, it is assumed that the citizens will be given the freedom to debate ideas and issues, as an essential part of their participation in the democratic process and the obligation to vote.

Answer (D) is a correct statement. Without freedom of speech, there is no democracy. In order to perform their obligation to vote and participate in the democratic process, the people must be free to express their opinions on important public issues.

1.11. In a democracy, the citizenry is free to make choices through their electoral choices. In other words, the citizenry can choose who to elect (or not to elect), and can express their views on the important issues of the day. In order for people to participate in the electoral process, they must be free to express themselves and their ideas to governmental officials, candidates, and on the issues of the day. In addition, the citizenry must have the freedom to try to persuade others to their positions. These facts are necessary to democratic self-government.

TOPIC 2:	ANSWERS
ADVOCACY OF ILLEGAL ACTION	

2.1.   **Answer (C) is correct.** This question tests knowledge of *Brandenburg v. Ohio*, 395 U.S. 444 (1969), which sets the modern rule on speech that advocates illegal action. *Brandenburg* allows government to punish speech seeking to incite illegal behavior. However, the *Brandenburg* test provides that incitement speech can be punished only when (1) the speaker intends to incite immediate illegal behavior and (2) that speech was likely in fact to produce that result. The facts suggest that Tom did not intend to incite an immediate riot, with the result that the first *Brandenburg* requirement is not met.

Answer (A) is incorrect because *Brandenburg* allows government to punish speech seeking to incite illegal behavior, even when that speech deals with core political issues.

Answer (B) is incorrect because the *Brandenburg* test provides that incitement speech can be punished only when (1) the speaker intends to incite immediate illegal behavior and (2) that speech was likely in fact to produce that result. Answer (B) misstates the rule.

Answer (D) is incorrect because incitement to riot does not require that the defendant actually have participated in the riot.

2.2.   **Answer (C) is correct** because it correctly states the rule from *Brandenburg v. Ohio*, 395 U.S. 444 (1969).

Answer (A) is incorrect as it states the rule of early 20th century cases such as *Abrams v. United States*, 250 U.S. 616 (1919) (speech that actually causes unlawful action can be punished as incitement), which has been superseded by *Brandenburg*.

Answer (B) is incorrect because it conflicts with *Brandenburg*.

Answer (D) is incorrect because under *Brandenburg* participation in the subsequent illegal conduct is irrelevant to whether the speech can be punished.

2.3.   **Answer (C) is correct** as the speaker satisfies the requirements from *Brandenburg v. Ohio*, 395 U.S. 444 (1969), *i.e.* that the speaker intend to incite immediate unlawful action and that there is a likelihood that the speaker will be successful.

Answer (A) is incorrect because the speaker's conduct fails the first *Brandenburg* requirement because his speech is abstract in nature.

Answer (B) is incorrect because the speaker's conduct fails the second *Brandenburg* requirement, since it seems likely he won't succeed in inciting the violence he is trying to incite.

Answer (D) is incorrect because, although the speaker seems close to satisfying *Brandenburg*, the violence happened several hours later. A court might determine that he was not the cause of the violence. *NAACP v. Claiborne Hardware*, 485 U.S. 886 (1982).

2.4.   The facts of this problem come directly from the case of *Brandenburg v. Ohio*, 395 U.S. 444 (1969). In *Brandenburg*, the Court concluded that these facts failed the "imminency" requirement and ultimately dismissed the case. A similar holding was rendered in *Virginia v. Black*, 538 U.S. 343 (2003). There was no indication that the organizers of the rally intended to encourage the participants to immediately engage in violence. As a result, the statements involve protected speech and are not prosecutable.

You might want to know whether participants in the rally in fact called for immediate lawless action, in an environment when such calls would likely to be heeded. For example, were potential targets nearby? Was the crowd roused and ready for action? Answers to this question might help illuminate whether the participants could be convicted consistent with *Brandenburg*.

3.1.   **Answer (A) is the statement that the Court did not make.** As we shall see (below), the Court did not say that the excluded categories of speech have no speech value whatsoever.

Answer (B) is a correct statement. The Court did say that the excluded categories of speech have such "slight value" towards the ascertainment of truth that they deserve no constitutional protection.

Answer (C) is a correct statement. In the list of categories of speech that have such slight value that they are not protected under the First Amendment, the Court included the lewd, the obscene, and the profane.

Answer (D) is a correct statement. In the list of categories of speech that have such slight social value that they are not protected under the First Amendment, the Court included libelous and insulting speech and fighting words.

3.2.   **Answer (B) is the statement that the Court did not make.** In other words, the Court did not state that fighting words are not constitutionally protected because they are insulting or because they offend basic concepts of human dignity.

Answer (A) is a statement that the Court did make. *Chaplinsky* suggested that fighting words are likely to provoke an immediate, violent response.

Answer (C) is a statement that the Court did make. *Chaplinsky* suggested that fighting words are likely to provoke an immediate response before reasoned discourse can occur.

Answer (D) is a statement that the Court did make. In the *Chaplinsky* decision, the Court stated that fighting words are not protected because they have only *slight* value in the marketplace of ideas.

3.3.   **Answer (C) is correct** because it suggests that offensive speech sometimes receives protection under the First Amendment. In fact, the Court tends to strike a middle ground which protects certain types of offensive speech, provided that they are not fighting words. *See Chaplinsky v. New Hampshire*, 315 U.S. 568 (1942); *see also Cohen v. California*, 403 U.S. 14 (1971) (protecting offensive speech in part because of its communicative value).

Answer (A) is incorrect because it states that offensive speech is unprotected under the First Amendment. In fact, cases like *Cohen v. California*, 403 U.S. 15 (1971), provide that so-called "offensive speech" sometimes receive special protection under the First Amendment.

Answer (B) is incorrect because it states that offensive speech always receives protection under the First Amendment. Even though offensive speech is often protected, it is not always protected. Some types of offensive speech (e.g., fighting words) receive no special protection under the First Amendment. *See Chaplinsky v. New Hampshire*, 315 U.S. 568 (1942).

Answer (D) is incorrect because, despite its offensive nature, such speech is sometimes protected. *See Cohen v. California, supra.*

3.4.   **Answer (D) is correct** because the Court did not hold that vulgar speech is unprotected. *See Cohen v. California*, 403 U.S. 15 (1971). On the contrary, the Court extended protecitons to such speech. *Id.*

Answer (A) is incorrect because *Cohen* held that a prohibition on "offensive speech" failed to put Cohen on notice that his conduct might be prohibited in a courthouse. *Id.*

Answer (B) is incorrect because *Cohen* held that a prohibition on "offensive speech" failed to put Cohen on notice that his conduct might be prohibited in a courthouse. *Id.*

Answer (C) is incorrect because the Court in *Cohen* was careful to consider the factual context surrounding the speech when determining if it was constitutionally protected. *Id.*

3.5.   In *Cohen v. California*, 403 U.S. 15 (1971), the Court held that speech should be protected as much for its emotive value as for its rational value:

[W]e cannot overlook the fact, because it is well illustrated by the episode involved here, that much linguistic expression serves a dual communicative function: it conveys not only ideas capable of relatively precise, detached explication, but otherwise inexpressible emotions as well. In fact, words are often chosen as much for their emotive as their cognitive force. We cannot sanction the view that the Constitution, while solicitous of the cognitive content of individual speech has little or no regard for that emotive function which practically speaking, may often be the more important element of the overall message sought to be communicated. Indeed, as Mr. Justice Frankfurter has said, "[o]ne of the prerogatives of American citizenship is the right to criticize public men and measures — and that means not only informed and responsible criticism but the freedom to speak foolishly and without moderation." *Baumgartner v. United States*, 322 U.S. 665, 673–674 (1944).

3.6.   **Answer (B) is correct** because the Court placed great weight on the invasive nature of broadcast media, and concluded that it could be "channeled" to times of the day when children were less likely to be listening. *See FCC v. Pacifica Foundation*, 438 U.S. 726 (1978).

Answer (A) is incorrect because the Court did not rely on *Cohen v. California*, 403 U.S. 15 (1971), to hold that the Carlin monologue was absolutely protected under the First Amendment. *Id.*

Answer (C) is incorrect because the Court upheld the FCC's authority to regulate this speech. *Id.*

Answer (D) is incorrect because the Court upheld the FCC's finding that its rules were violated.

3.7. **Answer (A) is correct.** In *National Endowment for the Arts v. Finley*, 524 U.S. 569 (1998), the Court upheld a congressional requirement that the National Endowment for the Arts (NEA) consider "general standards of decency and respect for the diverse beliefs and values of the American public" in making awards. In that case, the Court upheld the restriction: "That § 954(d)(1) admonishes the NEA merely to take 'decency and respect' into consideration, and that the legislation was aimed at reforming procedures rather than precluding speech, undercut respondents' argument that the provision inevitably will be utilized as a tool for invidious viewpoint discrimination."

Answer (B) is incorrect because *Finley* did not rely on *Cohen v. California*, 403 U.S. 15 (1971), to hold that Congress does not have the power to regulate so-called offensive speech.

Answer (C) is incorrect because the Court did not hold that Congress cannot mandate "general standards of decency."

Answer (D) is incorrect because the Court did not hold that Congress has broad power to proscribe indecent speech.

3.8. **Answer (B) is correct** because, in *Erznoznik v. City of Jacksonville*, 422 U.S. 205 (1975), the Court relied on *Cohen v. California*, and held that the burden normally falls upon the viewer to "avoid further bombardment of [his] sensibilities simply by averting [his] eyes."

Answer (A) is incorrect because the Court did hold that "offensive material" could be zoned to places where it would not be viewed by unwilling citizens, particularly children.

Answer (C) is incorrect because the Court explicitly relied on *Cohen* in reaching its decision.

Answer (D) is incorrect because the Court did not hold that municipalities have broad authority to regulate the content of drive-in movie theaters. Indeed, such a rule would run afoul of the Court's general disfavoring of content-based speech restrictions. *See, e.g., Police Dept of Chicago v. Mosley*, 408 U.S. 92 (1972).

3.9. In *Collin v. Smith*, 578 F.2d 1197 (7th Cir. 1978), the appellate court held that the City acted inappropriately in denying the parade permit:

> It would be grossly insensitive to deny, as we do not, that the proposed demonstration would seriously disturb, emotionally and mentally, at least some, and probably many of the Village's residents. The problem with engrafting an exception on the First Amendment for such situations is that they are indistinguishable in principle from speech that "invite(s) dispute . . . induces a condition of unrest, creates dissatisfaction with conditions as they are, or even stirs people to anger." *Terminiello v. Chicago*, 337 U.S. 1, 4 (1949). Yet these are among the "high purposes" of the First Amendment.

Id. It is perfectly clear that a state many not "make criminal the peaceful expression of unpopular views." *Edwards v. South Carolina*, 372 U.S. at 237. Likewise, "mere public intolerance or animosity cannot be the basis for abridgement of these constitutional freedoms." *Coates v. City of Cincinnati*, 402 U.S. 611, 615 (1971). Where, as here, a crime is made of a silent march, attended only by symbols and not by extrinsic conduct offensive in itself, we think the words of the Court in *Street v. New York*, 394 U.S. at 592, are very much on point:

> (A)ny shock effect . . . must be attributed to the content of the ideas expressed. It is firmly settled that under our Constitution the public expression of ideas may not be prohibited merely because the ideas are themselves offensive to some of their hearers.

3.10.   **Answer (A) is correct.** Under *Wisconsin v. Mitchell*, 508 U.S. 476 (1993), sentence enhancement schemes of the type in this question are not held to be violations of the First Amendment, because, according to the Supreme Court, such schemes penalize conduct, not thought.

Answer (B) is incorrect because the statute does not punish only thought. *Id.*

Answer (C) is incorrect, again, because of *Mitchell*. Because the statute does not penalize speech or thought, it makes no sense to speak of the statute as content- or viewpoint-based.

Answer (D) is incorrect, again, because the statute does not penalize thought.

3.11.   **Answer (A) is correct** because it reflects the analysis in *R.A.V. v. St. Paul*, 505 U.S. 377 (1992), where a similar ordinance was struck down because it was a content-based restriction on speech. Fighting words are not in themselves protected, which makes Answer (D) incorrect. However, the ordinance imposes a content-based restriction on such speech, which will be subject to strict scrutiny, and which can't survive that scrutiny, since a general intimidation or arson statute would take care of the problem

Answer (D) is incorrect because the Court has not held that fighting words are fully protected under the First Amendment.

Answer (B) is incorrect because the statute is content-based.

Answer (C) is incorrect for the same reason: because the ordinance is content-based it gets more scrutiny than would a general law proscribing all fighting words.

3.12.   On these facts, probably not. This question raises the issue of whether a hostile crowd can effectively silence a speaker by threatening to riot. In general, the Supreme Court has required a clear and present danger of incitement before a hostile crowd could successfully stop speech from occurring. *See* ERWIN CHEMERINSKY, CONSTITUTIONAL LAW: PRINCIPLES AND POLICIES 974 (2d ed. 2002). However, in later cases the Court has sometimes ruled in favor of speakers' rights on the theory that the police should have been expected to maintain control of the situation, given the facts of the particular case. *See, e.g., Edwards v. South*

Carolina, 372 U.S. 229 (1963). Here, with jeering but no threats of violence, a court would probably find there was not a clear and present danger of a riot, and would probably also find that the police could have been expected to keep control of the situation, at least unless and until it deteriorated further. Thus, Lee probably could not be validly convicted.

3.13.   **Answer (B) is correct** which reflects the Supreme Court's analysis in *Virginia v. Black*, 538 U.S. 343 (2003). In *Black*, the Court held that cross-burning has come to be seen as a general act of intimidation that is not necessarily limited to expression about racial issues. Thus, the Court held that a cross-burning statute was not content-based in the sense condemned by *R.A.V. v. St. Paul*, 505 U.S. 377 (1992).

Answer (A) is incorrect for the same reasons provided above.

Answer (C) is incorrect because the Court, in both *Black* and *R.A.V.*, made it clear that cross-burning is highly expressive.

Answer (D) is incorrect because the validity of the statute would turn either on how it was written or how it was enforced, not on whether Tom could show that he attempted to express an opinion on a particular topic.

3.14.   **Answer (B) is correct.** In *Chaplinksy v. New Hampshire*, 315 U.S. 568 (1942), the Court held that "fighting words" were unprotected because they "were no essential part in the expression of ideas." The facts in this case closely mirror those in *Chaplinksy*, where the Court allowed the conviction to stand.

Answer (A) is incorrect. The Court has not held that such speech is protected.

Answer (C) is incorrect because it goes too far. In *Cohen v. California*, 403 U.S. 15 (1971), the Court stated that in public areas people must be open to the possibility of hearing generally unpleasant words, and that government did not have the right to prohibit such words based on a concern for public decorum or decency.

Answer (D) is incorrect because Baker's motives and the validity of the officer's underlying conduct were both irrelevant to the question where his invective was constitutionally protected.

3.15.   **Answer (B) is correct.** It states the results from the Court's "hostile audience" jurisprudence. *See* ERWIN CHEMERINSKY, CONSTITUTIONAL LAW: PRINCIPLES AND POLICIES 821–24 (1st ed. 1997). Under that jurisprudence, the modern rule seems to be that the police must first try to control the hostile crowd; only if it cannot, and if the violence is imminent, can the police arrest the speaker.

Answer (A) is incorrect because under this approach the police would have too much leeway to arrest the speaker without having to take earlier steps.

Answer (C) is incorrect because it goes too far in the other direction; under current doctrine the police do have the power to arrest a speaker if he is unceasingly inciting a hostile crowd to violence.

Answer (D) is incorrect because under current doctrine it gives speech too little protection; if the police could require the speaker to tone down his words or face arrest, there would be significantly less First Amendment protection.

3.16. **Answer (B) is correct** because, prior to its holding in *New York Times Co. v. Sullivan*, 376 U.S. 254 (1964), the Court did not treat defamatory speech as protected speech. In *Chaplinsky v. New Hampshire*, 315 U.S. 568 (1942), the Court flatly stated that there are "certain well-defined and narrowly limited *classes* of speech, the prevention and punishment of which have never been thought to raise any Constitutional problem." *See Beauharnais v. Illinois*, 343 U.S. 250 (1952).

   Answer (A) is incorrect because, prior to *Sullivan*, the Court did not treat defamatory speech as protected speech. *See Chaplinsky v. New Hampshire, supra.*

   Answer (C) is incorrect. As previously indicated, prior to *Sullivan*, the Court did not hold that defamatory speech was entitled to full constitutional protection. *See Chaplinsky v. New Hampshire, supra.*

   Answer (D) is incorrect because the Court did not previously treat defamatory speech like political speech. *See Chaplinsky v. New Hampshire, supra.*

3.17. **Answer (A) is correct** because the states had broad authority to define the tort of defamation. *See New York Times Co. v. Sullivan*, 376 U.S. 254 (1964). Under decisions like *Chaplinsky v. New Hampshire*, 315 U.S. 568 (1942), the Court flatly stated that there are "certain well-defined and narrowly limited *classes* of speech, the prevention and punishment of which have never been thought to raise any Constitutional problem." As a result, the Constitution did not limit the authority of the states to define the tort of defamation.

   Answer (B) is incorrect because it provides that the states had no authority to define the tort of defamation, and (as previously indicated) the states had very broad authority. *See New York Times Co. v. Sullivan*, 376 U.S. 254 (1964).

   Answer (C) is incorrect because there were no federal laws limiting the power of the states to define the tort of defamation. *Id.*

   Answer (D) is incorrect because the states had broad authority to define the tort of defamation without regard to Congress' actions. *Id.*

3.18. **Answer (D) is correct** because *New York Times Co. v. Sullivan*, 376 U.S. 254 (1964), placed significant restrictions on the power of the states (including Alabama) to define the tort of defamation.

   Answer (A) is incorrect because *Sullivan* held that Alabama's defamation rules were unconstitutional. *Id.*

   Answer (B) is incorrect because *Sullivan* held that "[e]rroneous statement is inevitable in free debate, and [it] must be protected if the freedoms of expression are to have the 'breathing space' that they 'need [to] survive.' " *Id.*

   Answer (C) is incorrect because *Sullivan* held that "[i]njury to official reputation affords no more warrant for repressing speech that would otherwise be free than does factual error." *Id.*

3.19. In *New York Times Co. v. Sullivan*, 376 U.S. 254 (1964), the Court defined the "actual malice" standard in the following way:

> The constitutional guarantees require, we think, a federal rule that prohibits a public official from recovering damages for a defamatory falsehood relating to his official conduct unless he proves that the statement was made with "actual malice" — that is, with knowledge that it was false or with reckless disregard of whether it was false or not. . . .

3.20. **Answer (C) is correct** because *New York Times Co. v. Sullivan*, 376 U.S. 254 (1964), shifted the burden of proof to the public official plaintiff.

Answer (A) is incorrect because, although *Sullivan* is widely viewed as expressing skepticism regarding the role of the jury in the process of punishing defamatory speech (through the imposition of damages), the Court held that the jury could continue to hear such cases. *Id.*

Answer (B) is incorrect because, although *Sullivan* subjected public officials to the actual malice standard, it did not hold that they were barred from bringing defamation actions. *Id.*

Answer (D) is incorrect because it is the converse of Answer (C) which is correct. The burden of proof is on the plaintiff. *Id.*

3.21. In *New York Times Co. v. Sullivan*, 376 U.S. 254 (1964), the Court was heavily influenced by the impact of the historical crime of seditious libel. The Court stated that:

> If neither factual error nor defamatory content suffices to remove the constitutional shield from criticism of official conduct, the combination of the two elements is no less inadequate. This is the lesson to be drawn from the great controversy over the Sedition Act of 1798, which first crystallized a national awareness of the central meaning of the First Amendment. That statute made it a crime, punishable by a $5,000 fine and five years in prison, "if any person shall write, print, utter or publish [any] false, scandalous and malicious writing or writings against the government of the United States, or either house of the Congress[,] or the President[,] with intent to defame [or] to bring them, or either or any of them, into contempt or disrepute; or to excite against them, or either of any of them, the hatred of the good people of the United States." . . . Although the Sedition Act was never tested in this Court, the attack upon its validity has carried the day in the court of history. Fines levied in its prosecution were repaid by Act of Congress on the ground that it was unconstitutional. [There was] broad consensus that the Act, because of the restraint it imposed upon criticism of government and public officials, was inconsistent with the First Amendment. . . .
>
> What a State may not constitutionally bring about by means of a criminal statute is likewise beyond the reach of its civil law of libel. The fear of

damage awards under a rule such as that invoked by the Alabama courts here may be markedly more inhibiting than the fear of prosecution under a criminal statute.

3.22.   **Answer (C) is correct** because, in *New York Times Co. v. Sullivan*, 376 U.S. 254 (1964), the Court provided for independent review in a defamation case involving a public official and held that it must be sustained with "convincing clarity."

Answer (A) is incorrect because, in *Sullivan*, the Court made it clear that the defense of truth was not adequate to save the Alabama statute. *Id.*

Answer (B) is incorrect because the Court held that damages could not be presumed in a defamation case involving a public official. *Id.*

Answer (D) is incorrect because the Court did not address this issue. *Id.*

3.23.   **Answer (B) is correct** because *Curtis Publishing Co. v. Butts*, 388 U.S. 130 (1967), held that the actual malice standard should extend to public figures (as well as to the public officials to which it already applied).

Answer (A) is incorrect because, in *Curtis Publishing*, the Court did not abandon the actual malice standard as unworkable. *Id.*

Answer (C) is incorrect because *Curtis Publishing* did not hold that recovery could be based on simple negligence in some cases. *Id.*

Answer (D) is incorrect because *Curtis Publishing* did not adopt a "gross negligence" standard. *Id.*

3.24.   **Answers (D) is correct** because *Curtis Publishing Co. v. Butts*, 388 U.S. 130 (1967), did not suggest that the law has always treated public figures similarly to public officials.

Answer (A) is incorrect because *Curtis Publishing*'s holding is consistent with the notion that the public interest in reporting on public figures is as great as the public interest in reporting on public officials. *Id.*

Answer (B) is incorrect because *Curtis Publishing*'s holding is consistent with the idea that Butts had access to the media and could use that access to counter any false statements. *Id.*

Answer (C) is incorrect because *Curtis Publishing*'s holding is consistent with the notion that libel actions by public figures cannot be left to the dictates of state law without any constitutional protections. *Id.*

3.25.   **Answer (C) is correct** because *Gertz v. Robert Welch, Inc.*, 418 U.S. 323 (1974), held that private individuals should be distinguished from public officials and public figures, and subjected to lesser liability standards.

Answer (A) is incorrect because *Gertz* did not overrule *Curtis Publishing* and did not hold that lesser liability standards should be applied to public figures.

Answer (B) is incorrect because *Gertz* did not hold that lawyers should be subjected to the actual malice standard when they have some relationship to high profile criminal cases.

Answer (D) is incorrect because *Gertz* held that private individuals should be treated *differently* than public figures.

3.26. **Answer (D) is correct** because *Gertz* did not hold that private individuals deserve no constitutional protection.

Answer (A) is incorrect because *Gertz* held that the states have a legitimate interest in providing compensation to private individuals who have been defamed.

Answer (B) is incorrect because *Gertz* held that the actual malice standard exacts a high price from plaintiffs (making it more difficult for them to recover for injury to reputation) and this price might not be appropriate as applied to private individuals.

Answer (C) is incorrect because *Gertz* held that public officials and public figures have greater access to the media than private individuals, and therefore have the ability to exercise self-help by responding to defamation allegations.

3.27. **Answer (B) is correct** because *Gertz* held that "there can be no recovery of presumed or punitive damages, at least when liability is not based on a showing of knowledge of falsity or reckless disregard for the truth."

Answer (A) is incorrect because *Gertz* held that the states could not impose strict liability in these cases.

Answer (C) is incorrect because *Gertz* did not require private plaintiffs to show "gross negligence."

Answer (D) is incorrect because the Court did not hold that states could apply a liability without fault standard.

3.28. In *Gertz v. Robert Welch, Inc.*, 418 U.S. 323 (1974), the Court held that punitive damages are inappropriate in cases brought by private individuals for the following reasons:

> We also find no justification for allowing awards of punitive damages against publishers and broadcasters. . . . [J]uries assess punitive damages in wholly unpredictable amounts bearing no necessary relation to the actual harm caused. And they remain free to use their discretion selectively to punish expressions of unpopular views. Like the doctrine of presumed damages, jury discretion to award punitive damages [exacerbates] the danger of media self-censorship, [but] punitive damages are wholly irrelevant to the state interest that justifies a negligence standard for private defamation actions. They are not compensation for injury. Instead, they are private fines levied by civil juries to punish reprehensible conduct and to deter its future occurrence. In short, the private defamation plaintiff who establishes liability under a less demanding standard than that stated by *New York Times* may recover only such damages as are sufficient to compensate him for actual injury.

3.29.   **Answer (D) is correct** because *Dun & Bradstreet, Inc. v. Greenmoss Builders, Inc.*, 472 U.S. 749 (1985), held that presumed damages, but not punitive damages, may be awarded in favor of private plaintiffs.

Answer (A) is incorrect because *Dun* did not hold that gross negligence is required for the imposition of liability.

Answer (B) is incorrect because *Dun* did not hold that punitive damages may be awarded without any showing of fault.

Answer (C) is incorrect because *Dun* did not hold that strict liability may be imposed.

3.30.   **Answer (B) is correct** because *Hustler Magazine v. Falwell*, 485 U.S. 46 (1986), held that the actual malice standard should apply to intentional infliction cases.

Answer (A) is incorrect because *Hustler* did not hold that cases involving intentional infliction of mental and emotional distress should be treated differently than defamation cases.

Answer (C) is incorrect because *Hustler* did not hold that strict liability should be imposed in such cases.

Answer (D) is incorrect because *Hustler* did not hold that simple negligence provided an adequate basis for the imposition of liability in intentional infliction cases.

3.31.   In *Hustler Magazine v. Falwell*, 485 U.S. 46 (1988), the Court offered the following justifications for according special constitutional protection to ad parodies:

> Were we to hold otherwise, there can be little doubt that political cartoonists and satirists would be subjected to damages awards without any showing that their work falsely defamed its subject. . . . The appeal of the political cartoon or caricature is often based on exploitation of unfortunate physical traits or politically embarrassing events — an exploitation often calculated to injure the feelings of the subject of the portrayal. The art of the cartoonist is often not reasoned or evenhanded, but slashing and one-sided. One cartoonist expressed the nature of the art in these words: "The political cartoon is a weapon of attack, of scorn and ridicule and satire; it is least effective when it tries to pat some politician on the back. It is usually as welcome as a bee sting and is always controversial in some quarters." Long, The Political Cartoon: Journalism's Strongest Weapon, The Quill 56, 57 (Nov. 1962). Several famous examples of this type of intentionally injurious speech were drawn by Thomas Nast, probably the greatest American cartoonist to date, who was associated for many years during the post-Civil War era with Harper's Weekly. In the pages of that publication Nast conducted a graphic vendetta against William M. "Boss" Tweed and his corrupt associates in New York City's "Tweed Ring." It has been described by one historian of the subject as "a sustained attack which in its passion and effectiveness stands alone in the history of American

graphic art." M. KELLER, THE ART AND POLITICS OF THOMAS NAST 177 (1968). . . .

Despite their sometimes caustic nature, from the early cartoon portraying George Washington as an ass down to the present day, graphic depictions and satirical cartoons have played a prominent role in public and political debate. Nast's castigation of the Tweed Ring, Walt McDougall's characterization of Presidential candidate James G. Blaine's banquet with the millionaires at Delmonico's as "The Royal Feast of Belshazzar," and numerous other efforts have undoubtedly had an effect on the course and outcome of contemporaneous debate. . . . [O]ur political discourse would have been considerably poorer without them.

3.32. **Answer (C) is correct.** In *Stanley v. Georgia*, 394 U.S. 557 (1969), the Supreme Court protected the private possession and use of obscene material.

Answer (A) is incorrect because the "patently offensive" requirement is judged by reference to local standards. *Miller v. California*, 413 U.S. 15 (1973).

Answer (B) is incorrect because *Miller* imposes no requirement of a showing of harm to the community before alleged obscenity can be suppressed.

Answer (D) is incorrect because *Miller* also requires that the material must be fairly classifiable as "hard core" pornography, thus introducing a national "floor" to what may satisfy the "patently offensive" standard.

3.33. Under *Roth v. United States*, 354 U.S. 476 (1957), obscenity is not protected by the Constitution. However, this book may not be obscene under the standard set forth in *Miller v. California*, 413 U.S. 15 (1973). In particular, *Miller* requires that a jury find that the work in question be patently offensive under the state law defining obscenity, and appeal primarily to the prurient interest, using contemporary community standards. However, *Miller* also requires that the work be without serious artistic, literary, political, or scientific value, taken as a whole and using a national standard. Here, the fact that cultural commentators have praised the book, and that it was nominated for several book awards, suggests that it probably has serious value and thus is not obscene.

3.34. **Answer (D) is correct** because this judgment is based on a national standard. *Pope v. Illinois*, 481 U.S. 497 (1987).

Answer (A) is incorrect because this judgment is based on a national standard. *Pope v. Illinois*, 481 U.S. 497 (1987).

Answer (B) is incorrect because a judicial check is available when a jury finds that a work is patently offensive. *Jenkins v. Georgia*, 418 U.S. 153 (1974).

Answer (C) is incorrect because a minimal mention of a literary, artistic, political, or scientific issue will not immunize a work. *Miller v. California*, 413 U.S. 15 (1973); A. IDES & CHRISTOPHER MAY, CONSTITUTIONAL LAW: EXAMPLES AND EXPLANATIONS, INDIVIDUAL RIGHTS (3d ed.) 353.

3.35. **Answer (A) is correct.** Beginning with its decision in *Roth v. United States*, 354 U.S. 476 (1957), the Court has consistently held that obscenity lacks First Amendment protection. *See* ERWIN CHEMERINSKY, CONSTITUTIONAL LAW: PRINCIPLES AND POLICIES 982 (2d ed. 2002); *see also Miller v. California*, 413 U.S. 15 (1973)..

Answer **(B) is incorrect** because the Court has not vacillated on this issue. Despite dissents, a majority has consistently held obscenity to be unprotected. *E.g., Roth; Miller.*

Answer **(C) is incorrect** because the Court has not held that obscenity enjoys First Amendment protection, although a lesser amount than the protection enjoyed by core political speech. *Id.*

Answer **(D) is incorrect** because the Court, which previously held that obscenity lacked First Amendment protection, did not settle on a view under which obscenity enjoys First Amendment protection, although a lesser amount than the protection enjoyed by core political speech. Instead, obscenity continues to be unprotected. *Id.*

3.36. **Answer (B) is correct** because, in *Stanley v. Georgia*, 394 U.S. 557 (1969), the Supreme Court held that private possession of obscenity cannot be criminalized. However, in *Paris Adult Theater I v. Slaton*, 413 U.S. 49 (1973), the Court held that sale, distribution, and exhibition of such material can be prohibited. The correct combination of these two holdings is reflected in Answer (B).

Answer **(A) is incorrect** because *Stanley* did not hold that the government may prohibit the possession of obscenity in the home.

Answer **(C) is incorrect** because *Stanley* did not hold that government may neither prohibit its possession in the home nor its sale, distribution, or exhibition in public, as long as that sale, distribution, or exhibition is to interested and consenting parties in a place shielded from the public at large.

Answer **(D) is incorrect** because *Stanley* did not hold that government may prohibit obscenity in any and all contexts.

4.1.   **Answer (C) is the correct answer.** In creating new categories of excluded speech, the Court has sometimes focused on the societal interest in prohibiting that particular type of speech. *See, e.g., New York v. Ferber*, 458 U.S. 747 (1982) (noting the damage to children as a major part of the rationale for banning non-obscene child pornography).

    Answer (A) is incorrect. In creating these new categories of unprotected speech, the Court has not consistently followed the *Chaplinsky* approach to categorical exclusions of speech.

    Answer (B) is also incorrect. In creating these new categories of excluded speech, the Court has not focused *solely* on the speech value (*e.g.*, does it have only "slight value" towards ascertainment of the truth) of the particular category of speech. *See, e.g., Ferber*. However, the value of the speech has sometimes been considered a factor in the analysis.

    Answer (D) is incorrect. In creating these new categories of unprotected speech, the Court has not explicitly rejected the *Chaplinsky* approach as outdated and inappropriate.

4.2.   **Answer (C) is correct.** In recent years, the intermediate scrutiny test from *Central Hudson Gas v. Pub. Serv. Comm'n*, 447 U.S. 557 (1980), has been interpreted to give more and more protection to free speech concerns. *See, e.g., Thompson v. Western States Medical Center*, 535 U.S. 357 (2002).

    Answer (A) is incorrect. In past years the Court has suggested that this intermediate level of scrutiny, when combined with government's power to regulate the underlying transaction, gives the government the power to take the lesser step of banning the underlying transaction. *Posadas of Puerto Rico Assn v. Tourism Co.*, 478 U.S. 328 (1985). However, that view has been rejected in recent years. *See 44 Liquormart v. Rhode Island*, 517 U.S. 484 (1996).

    Answer (B) is incorrect. Ostensibly, commercial speech continues to enjoy on the intermediate scrutiny given it in *Central Hudson*.

    Answer (D) is incorrect because the Court has not given commercial speech the lowest level of protection. *See Central Hudson; 44 Liquormart v. Rhode Island*, 517 U.S. 484 (1996).

4.3.   **Answer (D) is correct.** In *Virginia Bd. of Pharmacy v. Virginia Citizens Consumer Council*, 425 U.S. 748 (1976), the Court expressed each of the first three of these rationales for protecting commercial speech. However, it did not express the fourth. Nor could it, in *Virginia Board* or any subsequent opinion; most commercial transactions that are the subject of commercial speech can be heavily regulated by the government without running afoul of the Constitution. *See Carolene Products v. United States*, 304 U.S. 144 (1938) (setting forth deferential test for due process challenges to regulation of commercial transaction).

Answer (A) is incorrect because the Court has, in fact, held that commercial speech allows consumers in a free market to make wise choices. *See Virginia Bd. of Pharmacy v. Virginia Citizens Consumer Council*, 425 U.S. 748 (1976).

Answer (B) is incorrect because the Court has, in fact, held that commercial speech speaks to issues citizens may care deeply about. *Id.*

Answer (C) is incorrect because the Court has, in fact, held that much speech that is traditionally thought to have been protected has been commercial in nature. *Id.* (citing books and motion pictures).

4.4.   **Answer (D) is correct** because it incorrectly states the law (and thus is the correct answer here). The Court does not give government more power to restrict speech when it has the power to regulate the underlying transaction. *44 Liquormart v. Rhode Island*, 517 U.S. 484 (1996).

Answer (A) is incorrect because under *Central Hudson Gas v. Public Service Comm'n*, 447 U.S. 557 (1980), which set forth the current test for commercial speech regulation, protected speech must not be misleading.

Answer (B) is incorrect because commercial speech only received First Amendment protection in *Virginia Bd. of Pharmacy v. Virginia Citizens Consumer Council*, 425 U.S. 748 (1976). *Compare Valentine v. Chrestensen*, 316 U.S. 52 (1942) (denying protection to commercial speech).

Answer (C) is incorrect because the *Central Hudson* test has been described as an "intermediate scrutiny" test. *Florida Bar v. Went for It, Inc.*, 515 U.S. 618 (1995).

4.5.   **Answer (A) is correct** because it reflects the Court's statements in cases such as *Virginia Bd. of Pharmacy v. Virginia Citizens Consumer Council*, 517 U.S. 484 (1976) and *City of Cincinnati v. Discovery Networks*, 507 U.S. 410 (1993).

Answer (B) is incorrect because it is too broad, as it would include things such as films put out by motion picture studios, which do not automatically count as commercial speech. *Joseph Burstyn, Inc. v. Wilson*, 343 U.S. 495 (1952).

Answer (C) is incorrect. This statement is too broad since motion picture studios and newspapers are commercial entities but their speech gets more protection than does commercial speech. *E.g., New York Times v. Sullivan*, 517 U.S. 484 (1964).

Answer (D) is incorrect because it is too narrow; all types of advertising are commercial speech. *44 Liquormart v. Rhode Island*, 517 U.S. 484 (1996) (price placards at a store).

4.6.   **Answer (B) is correct** because it most accurately states the law of unconstitutional conditions and free speech. In *Rust v. Sullivan*, 500 U.S. 173 (1991), the Court observed that the program was a government-created one that the government had a right to insist it convey a particular message.

Answer (A) is incorrect because in *Rust*, the Court allowed the government to restrict the speech of doctors who were practicing pursuant to a federally-funded pre-natal care program.

Answer (C) is incorrect because it allows the government too much latitude to restrict speech. *See* ERWIN CHEMERINSKY, CONSTITUTIONAL LAW: PRINCIPLES AND POLICIES 795–800 (1st ed. 1997).

Answer (D) is incorrect because it also imposes too few restrictions on government, which is inconsistent with the caselaw. *See* CHEMERINSKY, *supra*.

4.7. **Answer (C) is correct.** In *American Booksellers Ass'n v. Hudnut*, 771 F.2d 323 (7th Cir. 1985), *aff'd*, 475 U.S. 1001 (1986), the appellate court struck down an ordinance like this one, on the ground that it was a content-based speech restriction, and the Supreme Court affirmed without an opinion. Given the Supreme Court's affirmation, it is likely that a court would use the same reasoning to strike down this law as well.

Answer (A) is incorrect because content-based restrictions on speech are so heavily disfavored, even when the speech is not particularly valuable. *See R.A.V. v. St. Paul*, 505 U.S. 377 (1992).

Answer (B) is incorrect because the statute is content-based, which makes the statute not valid as a time, place, or manner restriction. *See* ERWIN CHEMERINSKY, CONSTITUTIONAL LAW: PRINCIPLES AND POLICIES 924 (1st ed. 1997).

Answer (D) is incorrect because, under *R.A.V.*, even unprotected speech cannot be regulated in a content-based way unless the restriction satisfies strict scrutiny.

4.8. **Answer (B) is correct.** The Court faced a similar situation in *United States v. Playboy Entertainment Group*, 529 U.S. 803 (2000), where it applied strict scrutiny to a statute similar to this one.

Answer (A) is incorrect because even though the Court agreed that protecting children was a compelling government interest, the content-based nature of the restriction led the Court to impose strict scrutiny.

Answer (C) is incorrect because, while there may be some spectrum scarcity in cable, thus justifying some government content regulation, that justification is not as strong as in the broadcast context, where the scarcity problem is thought to be even worse. *Turner Broadcasting v. F.C.C.*, 512 U.S. 662 (1994).

Answer (D) is incorrect because strict scrutiny puts the burden of proof on the government, not the plaintiff. *Playboy Entertainment Group, supra*.

4.9. **Answer (C) is correct.** In *Ginsberg v. New York*, 393 U.S. 503 (1968), the Court upheld a similar statute based on this analysis.

Answer (A) is incorrect because children have at least some First Amendment rights. *Tinker v. Des Moines Sch. Dist.*, 393 U.S. 503 (1969).

Answer (B) is incorrect, based on *Ginsberg*'s analysis.

Answer (D) is incorrect. *Ginsberg* did not require that a court make an individualized determination of the sort described in this answer.

4.10.   **Answer (B) is correct.** In *Buckley v. Valeo*, 424 U.S. 1 (1976), the Court held that contributions, while speech, are nevertheless subject to amount regulations on the theory that contributions simply represent symbolic joining with the candidate, which can be accomplished through contributions of limited size.

Answer (A) is incorrect because *Buckley* held that the attenuated speech value of contributions means that restrictions are not subject to the highest scrutiny.

Answer (C) is incorrect because *Buckley* and cases like it concede that such contributions are still speech.

Answer (D) is incorrect because *Buckley* and cases like it concede that contributions are speech, even when made by someone other than the candidate herself.

4.11.   **Answer (B) is correct** because it states the Supreme Court's view since *Buckley v. Valeo* 424 U.S. 1 (1976).

Answer (A) is incorrect because cases such as *Buckley* have concluded that direct expenditures come closer to actual speech than campaign contributions.

Answer (C) is incorrect. *Buckley* and subsequent cases have considered expenditures on behalf of candidates as core political speech, not simply commercial speech that receives less than full First Amendment protection.

Answer (D) is incorrect because the fact that direct expenditures come close to actual speech (*see Buckley*) makes restrictions on them a problem under the First Amendment.

4.12.   **Answer (C) is correct.** It reflects the Supreme Court's statement in *Citizens Against Rent Control v. Berkeley*, 454 U.S. 290 (1981), that the same protections for direct expenditures in electoral campaigns apply to referendum campaigns as well.

Answer (A) is incorrect because *Citizens Against Rent Control* did not suggest that a court should impose a lesser level of scrutiny on limitations of direct expenditures on referendum as on electoral campaigns.

Answer (B) is incorrect because *Citizens Against Rent Control* did not hold that a referendum campaign's relationship to direct democracy meant that stricter scrutiny should be applied to direct expenditure limitations on referendum campaigns.

Answer (D) is incorrect because strict scrutiny applies to restrictions on direct expenditures in referendum campaigns, thus making it unlikely that the Court would uphold such restrictions.

4.13.   The contribution limits would probably be upheld, but not the expenditure limits. In *Buckley v. Valeo*, 424 U.S. 1 (1976), the Court held that campaign contributions are a form of speech. However, because such speech is more symbolic — the act of giving money conveys support of a candidate — the size of contributions can be restricted without infringing on the communicative aspect of contributing. *Buckley* upheld significantly lower contribution limits than the ones in this question, even accounting for inflation since 1976. It is likely this contribution limit would survive as well.

However, *Buckley* distinguished expenditures, which are the speaker's own explicit speech. Indeed, as political speech, such speech is at the core of the First Amendment. For these reasons, restrictions on direct expenditures for speech — whether made by a citizen or by the candidate herself — are subject to strict judicial scrutiny. Such restrictions were struck down in *Buckley*, with the Court rejecting the argument that they were justified by the government interest in combating the reality or appearance of corruption, and the argument that the restrictions were necessary to ease pressure on candidates to fundraise. It is likely they would continue to be held insufficient. *See Citizens United v. Federal Election Comm'n*, 130 S. Ct. 876 (2010) (rejecting corruption arguments as justifications for limitations on corporate political expenditures).

4.14.   **Answer (A) is correct** because it restates the result and reasoning in *Davis v. Federal Election Comm'n*, 128 S. Ct. 2759 (2008).

Answer (B) is incorrect because it is too broad: a number of cases have upheld limits on campaign contributions, including the seminal case of *Buckley v. Valeo*, 424 U.S. 1 (1976).

Answer (C) is incorrect because it states the view of the dissenters in *Davis*.

Answer (D) is incorrect because it states the wrong result but also because it gets the law backwards: contribution restrictions are generally more likely to be upheld than spending restrictions.

4.15.   **Answer (A) is correct.** Answer (C) would have been correct until 2010, but in *Citizens United v. Federal Election Comm'n*, 130 S. Ct. 876 (2010), the Court overruled *Austin v. Michigan Chamber of Commerce*, 494 U.S. 652 (1990), which would have supported upholding the law. *Citizens United* held that a federal restriction on corporations' spending of its general treasury funds on electoral advocacy, and restricting such expenditures to a political action committee, or "PAC", funded by shareholders and managers of the corporation, did not satisfy strict scrutiny and was unconstitutional. The result would probably be the same here.

Answer (B) is incorrect because direct expenditures in general do enjoy a high degree of constitutional protection, under *Buckley v. Valeo*, 424 U.S. 1 (1976).

Answer (C) is incorrect. It reflects the reasoning of the Supreme Court in *Austin v. Michigan Chamber of Commerce*, 494 U.S. 652 (1990). In *Austin*, the Court reasoned that because the corporate form allows the accumulation of large amounts of capital, and because shareholders may or may not share in the political views of corporate management, government had more leeway to restrict direct expenditures by corporations, as compared with expenditures by private parties. However, *Austin* was overruled in *Citizens United*.

Answer (D) is incorrect because those special problems might cut in favor of, not against, of the constitutionality of regulation, at least under *Austin*. But this issue is moot, given *Citizens United*.

4.16. **Answer (D) is correct.** In *Buckley v. American Constitutional Law Foundation*, 525 U.S. 182 (1999), the Supreme Court stated that a requirement such as the one in Answer (D) could legitimately be imposed by a state.

Answer (A) is incorrect because in *Meyer v. Grant*, 486 U.S. 414 (1988), the Court struck down a prohibition on paying signature gatherers, on the ground that it inhibited the ability of referendum sponsors to express their viewpoints.

Answer (B) is incorrect. In *Buckley*, the Court applied strict scrutiny and struck down requirements such as those in Answers (B).

Answer (C) is incorrect because *Buckley* suggests Utopia could not require that the petition signature gatherers be registered voters in Utopia.

4.17. **Answer (B) is correct.** This idea was explicitly rejected in *Buckley v. Valeo*, 424 U.S. 1 (1976), and since then a majority of the Supreme Court has never explicitly embraced it.

Answer (A) is incorrect because in *Nixon v. Shrink Missouri Government PAC*, 528 U.S. 377 (2000), the Court stated that combating the reality and the appearance of corruption through campaign contribution limits was a legitimate government interest.

Answer (C) is incorrect because in *Buckley* the Court noted the constitutional protection enjoyed by direct expenditures in favor of a candidate.

Answer (D) is incorrect because in *First National Bank of Boston v. Bellotti*, 435 U.S. 765 (1978), the Court recognized that corporations, like other organizations, have at least some rights to participate in the political process. These rights were reaffirmed and potentially expanded in *Citizens United v. Federal Election Comm'n*, 130 S. Ct. 876 (2010).

4.18. **Answer (A) is correct.** In *Pickering v. Board of Education*, 391 U.S. 563 (1968), the Court enunciated this basic balancing test. The Court in *Pickering* recognized the importance of the government's interest as an employer, but also noted the citizen's interest in speaking on matters of public concern.

Answer (B) is incorrect because it is inconsistent with the holding in *Pickering*.

Answer (C) is incorrect because *Pickering* noted that an individual's First Amendment rights were only part of a balance that had to be struck in each case.

Answer (D) is incorrect because in *Connick v. Myers*, 461 U.S. 138 (1983), the Court, in ruling against the employee, focused on the fact that the speech in that case was not on a matter of public concern, a factor that has since become part of the standard *Pickering* balancing approach.

4.19.   A court would probably rule against the attorney. In general, questions about the speech rights of government employees are answered by the following approach. First, the employee must prove that that the adverse employment action was motivated by the employee's speech. If he can prove this, and if the speech is on a matter of public concern, the court must then balance the employee's speech rights against the government's interest in the efficient functioning of the office. *See* ERWIN CHEMERINSKY, CONSTITUTIONAL LAW: PRINCIPLES AND POLICIES 1071 (2d ed. 2002).

In *Connick v. Myers*, 461 U.S. 138 (1983), a case factually close to this hypothetical, the Court held that an assistant D.A.'s memo dealing with transfer policies and morale issues was not on a matter of public concern, largely because the attorney was not attempting to inform the public and because the Court considered the speech to be more about a simple employment dispute. But note that lack of public dissemination of the information is not always enough to doom the First Amendment claim; for example, in *Givhan v. Western Line Consolidated Sch. Dist.*, 439 U.S. 410 (1979), privately-communicated speech about a school's alleged racial discrimination was held to be protected, such that a firing based on that speech was unconstitutional. In *Connick*, though, speech about the efficient functioning of a government office, even one like the D.A., was held sufficiently private, especially when not communicated to the public, as to deny the speaker First Amendment protection when that speech got him fired.

4.20.   **Answer (B) is correct**, because it reflects the Court's resolution of a similar issue in *Rankin v. McPherson*, 483 U.S. 378 (1987). In *Rankin* the Court noted the private nature of the conversation (between the speaker and another co-worker), which was relevant to whether the speech disrupted the workplace. It also noted that the speaker, while working in a constable's office, was a civilian employee.

Answer (A) is incorrect because in *Rankin*, the Court did not adopt such an approach to an analogous comment; more generally, the balancing required is context-specific, thus making such blanket statements inaccurate.

Answer (C) is incorrect because it is similarly too broad; since *Pickering v. Board of Education*, 391 U.S. 563 (1968), the Court has required a more context-sensitive balancing, respecting the government's interest in efficient operation.

Answer (D) is incorrect because it reflects Justice Holmes' famous dictum from *McAuliffe v. Mayor of New Bedford*, 29 N.E. 517 (1892), that one may have a right to free speech but not a right to a government job. That dictum, however, is not good law in light of *Pickering* and *Connick*.

4.21.   Probably not. In *City of Renton v. Playtime Theatres, Inc.*, 475 U.S. 41 (1986), the Court upheld a similar ordinance. The Court specifically rejected the argument that such a zoning law should be struck down because it made the exercise of such speech significantly more expensive. The Court required only that adult theaters be given a reasonable chance to operate. The fact that the real estate market in the locality made the space legally accessible to him undesirable did not have any constitutional significance. Thus, here, also, the statute probably gives the speaker all the opportunity to speak that the Constitution requires.

4.22. Probably not. While music is speech and thus is protected by the First Amendment, *see Ward v. Rock Against Racism*, 491 U.S. 781 (1989), the ordinance is a classic time, place, and manner regulation and would probably survive First Amendment scrutiny. The requirements for a valid time, place, or manner regulation is that it be content-neutral, serve an important government interest and leave open adequate alternative places for expression. *See* Erwin Chemerinsky, Constitutional Law: Principles and Policies 1092 (2d ed. 2002). Here, the ordinance is probably content-neutral; it is not aimed at loud music because of disagreement with any particular message conveyed by the loudness (indeed, this is borne out by the fact that loud music is barred only at certain times, and is allowed later in the night on weekends). Maintenance of the peace and quiet of a neighborhood is clearly an important government interest. Finally, the later cut-off point for louder music on weekends, plus the fact that music in general is allowed any time the bar can be open, probably means that there is an adequate alternative avenue for the bar owner to express himself via the bands he books. For these reasons the ordinance is probably constitutional.

4.23. The ordinance would probably be upheld. The first question to ask is whether the airport is a public forum. Unless the City of Chicago designated the airport as a public forum (highly unlikely), the answer to that question is probably "no." In *International Society for Krishna Consciousness v. Lee*, 505 U.S. 672 (1992), the case on which this problem is modeled, the Supreme Court held that an airport was not a traditional public forum, as it was not a place that, from time immemorial, had been used for speech. If O'Hare Airport is not a public forum, then government regulation of speech there may be content-based, as long as it is viewpoint-neutral and reasonable. Here, the restriction is content-based, in that it bans solicitation speech but not other speech (e.g., proselytizing speech). But it is viewpoint-neutral, as it bans all solicitation speech. A court would probably also find the restriction to be reasonable; in *Lee* the Court held that concerns about fraud and harassment of busy passengers justified a ban on solicitation speech. For these reasons the ordinance would probably be upheld.

4.24. **Answer (A) is correct.** Because cross burning was associated with the Klu Klux Klan, and its historical efforts to intimidate through violence, the Court in *Black* held that cross burning can be prohibited when it is being used as a method for intimidating someone else.

Answer (B) is incorrect. Cross burning is not regarded as so pernicious that it can always be prohibited. *Black* suggested that it can only be prohibited when associated with threats and intimidation.

Answer (C) is incorrect. The Court has not held that that cross burning can be prohibited because the cross is regarded as a sacred symbol. There are no sacred symbols that they are beyond the protection of free speech under the First Amendment.

Answer (D) is incorrect. It is not accurate to state that cross burning can never be prohibited under any circumstances. As noted in the prior answer, there are circumstances in which it can be prohibited.

5.1.   **Answer (B) is correct.** Speech on private property is protected, and government is limited in its ability to regulate it. *See United States v. Playboy Entertainment Group*, 529 U.S. 803 (2000). Government has significant latitude to restrict speech on government-owned property used for government's own purposes (rather than for speech). *Greer v. Spock*, 424 U.S. 828 (1976). However, government is restricted in its ability to restrict speech on public property either traditionally given over to speech, *Schneider v. New Jersey*, 307 U.S. 496 (1939), or dedicated to speech, *Widmar v. Vincent*, 454 U.S. 263 (1981).

   Answer (A) is incorrect because government has limited latitude to restrict speech on private property. *See Playboy.*

   Answer (C) is incorrect because the government does not have equal latitude to restrict speech on all property. In fact, the government's authority varies depending on the context. *See Playboy.*

   Answer (D) is incorrect because government does not have broad latitude to restrict speech on private property. *See Playboy.*

5.2.   **Answer (A) is correct.** A public forum can either be one traditionally open to speech, *Schneider v. New Jersey*, 307 U.S. 496 (1939), or one government has dedicated to speech, *Widmar v. Vincent*, 454 U.S. 263 (1981).

   Answer (B) is incorrect. In *International Society for Krishna Consciousness v. Lee*, 505 U.S. 672 (1992), the Court rejected a claim that an airport was a public forum, adopting a restrictive understanding of what constitutes traditional public forums.

   Answer (C) is incorrect because areas may be non-public forums that are nevertheless open to non-employees, *e.g.*, *United States v. Kokinda*, 497 U.S. 720 (1990) (post office sidewalks).

   Answer (D) is incorrect because it is too broad a definition of public forum, and it misses the focus on whether the area was traditionally open or whether it was dedicated to expression. For example, in *Adderly v. Florida*, 385 U.S. 39 (1966), the Court held that the area outside prisons is not a public forum, despite the fact that protests against jailings could most effectively take place in front of prisons.

5.3.   **Answer (C) is correct** as it states the result and reasoning in *Pleasant Grove City v. Summum*, 129 S. Ct. 1125 (2009), whose facts are closely analogous to the ones in this question.

   Answer (A) is incorrect because the Court in *Summum* held that monuments in parks constituted government speech, thus making the content-neutrality requirement inapplicable.

Answer (B) is incorrect for the same reason as answer (A), and also because it misstates the standard of review for content-based restrictions.

Answer (D) is incorrect because it is too broad; for example, a demonstration in a park would not constitute government speech just because it occurred on government property.

5.4.   **Answer (B) is correct.** It correctly reflects the result in *Boos v. Barry*, 485 U.S. 312 (1988), which considered an analogous statute. The Court in *Boos* held that the sign provision was content-based, and thus received strict scrutiny (which it failed) because it was imposed on speech on sidewalks, a traditional public forum. The Court also held that the dispersal provision was not necessarily unconstitutional, since it was unrelated to the content of speech.

Answer (A) is incorrect. A content-neutral speech restriction on speech in a public forum may be upheld if it satisfies the relatively deferential time, place and manner test.

Answer (C) is incorrect because a content-based restriction on speech in a public forum must be quite narrowly drawn to further a legitimate government interest (*Boos*); here, the concern for international goodwill might have been furthered through less restrictive means.

Answer (D) is incorrect because, as noted in *Boos*, sidewalks are traditional public forums, which presumptively opens them up for speech activities.

5.5.   **Answer (B) is correct.** In *Marsh v. Alabama*, 326 U.S. 501 (1946), the Supreme Court held that a corporate owner of a company-owned town had to allow speakers on the sidewalks of that town, just as any municipality would. The Court extended this holding to shopping malls in *Amalgamated Food Employees Union v. Logan Valley Plaza*, 391 U.S. 308 (1968). But in *Lloyd Corp. v. Tanner*, 407 U.S. 551 (1972) the Court cut back on *Logan Valley*, and in *Hudgens v. NLRB*, 424 U.S. 507 (1976), the Court overruled *Logan Valley* entirely, although *Marsh* remains good law. This history is reflected in Answer (B), which makes it the correct answer.

Answer (A) is incorrect because the history recounted above demonstrates that in the past, shopping centers were subject to the First Amendment.

Answer (C) is incorrect because under *Hudgens* there is no chance for Andy to win even if he makes the showing described in the answer.

Answer (D) is incorrect because *Hudgens* overruled *Logan Valley*.

5.6.   **Answer (B) is correct.** Political speech is at the core of the First Amendment (*Buckley v. Valeo*, 424 U.S. 1 (1976)), but all speech is subject to valid time, place, and manner regulations (*Ward v. Rock Against Racism*, 491 U.S. 781 (1989)). Answer (B) is correct, since under *Ward*, time, place, and manner regulations must be content-neutral and allow some way for the speaker to make the speech he wishes to make, conditions that are satisfied here since the restriction applies to all sound trucks but allows them to be used from 8:00 a.m. to 8:00 p.m.

Answer (A) is incorrect; even though political speech is at the core of the First Amendment, speech in general may be subject to reasonable time, place and manner restrictions. *See also Kovacs*, discussed below.

Answer (C) is incorrect because there is no exception from time, place and manner regulations for speech on matters of great public interest. *Kovacs v. Cooper*, 366 U.S. 77 (1949) (sound truck used to comment on labor dispute subject to time, place and manner restrictions).

Answer (D) is incorrect because the campaign finance laws considered by the Court have not dealt with the manner of speaking, except to the extent that they deal with television and other electronic media (*e.g., McConnell v. FEC*, 540 U.S. 93 (2003); *but see Citizens United v. Federal Election Comm'n*, 130 S. Ct. 876 (2010) (overruling part of *McConnell*)).

5.7.   **Answer (B) is correct** because the fact that they must be content-neutral means that the Court's ends-means scrutiny is relatively deferential. *Ward v. Rock Against Racism*, 491 U.S. 781 (1989).

Answer (A) is incorrect. It is partly right, but in *Ward*, the Court made clear that the narrow tailoring referred to in the standard was not the same kind of tight-fit requirement that narrow tailoring is in other contexts. Rather, the *Ward* Court described it in much more deferential terms, making Answer (B) correct.

Answer (C) is incorrect because they must be both content-neutral and viewpoint-neutral. *Ward v. Rock Against Racism.* Indeed, it is difficult to conceive of a restriction that is content-neutral but viewpoint-based.

Answer (D) is incorrect. A valid time, place, or manner restriction must be content-neutral; by definition, that means it also must be viewpoint-neutral. *Ward v. Rock Against Racism.*

5.8.   **Answer (A) is correct.** That answer reflects the Court's analysis in *Texas v. Johnson*, 491 U.S. 397 (1989), where the Court found a similar statute to be an attempt by a state to prevent flag burning to communicate dissent. This analysis is reflected in Answer (A), which states that the statute clearly bans flag burning except when done in a way respectful to it; this makes it a viewpoint-based restriction on speech.

Answer (B) is incorrect because it states the position of the dissent in *Johnson*.

Answer (C) is incorrect because under *Johnson*, burning a flag comes under the category of symbolic speech, that is, conduct that is performed in order to express a particular idea. Symbolic speech is protected by the First Amendment. *See also United States v. O'Brien*, 391 U.S. 367 (1968) (draft card burning is expression that enjoys at least some First Amendment protection).

Answer (D) is incorrect because it goes too far; a content-neutral restriction on speech may be constitutional under a time, place, or manner analysis. *See* ERWIN CHEMERINSKY, CONSTITUTIONAL LAW: PRINCIPLES AND POLICIES 924–25 (1st ed. 1997).

5.9. **Answer (B) is correct** In *New York Times v. Sullivan*, 517 U.S. 484 (1971), the Court allowed publication of the Pentagon Papers, secret Defense Department documents relating to the Vietnam War, despite a government request for a prior restraint. In so doing, the Court enunciated the very high standard required for issuing such a restraint, as expressed in Answer (B).

Answer (A) is incorrect. The standard in *New York Times* is much higher than that expressed in Answer (A), which makes that answer wrong.

Answer (C) is incorrect because under *New York Times*, the possibility of penalizing the publisher after publication does not make the case for a prior restraint significantly stronger.

Answer (D) is incorrect. The *New York Times* Court was careful to say that there was not an absolute prohibition on prior restraints.

5.10. **Answer (B) is correct.** In *City of Renton v. Playtime Theaters*, 475 U.S. 41 (1986), the Court enunciated a deferential approach to speech regulation that was justified as an attempt to mitigate the bad secondary effects of speech. That approach deferred to the city's statement that the regulation was not motivated by content, and was largely unconcerned that the particularities of the real estate market were such that the ordinance did not leave a lot of desirable space open for the speech. This deferential approach is reflected in Answer (B).

Answer (A) is incorrect because the *City of Renton*'s approach held that such regulations were not content based.

Answer (C) is incorrect because *City of Renton*'s approach was not overly concerned with the exigencies of the real estate market and how that affected the speaker's ability to speak.

Answer (D) is incorrect because such speech does enjoy some constitutional protection, under *Miller v. California*, 413 U.S. 15 (1973).

5.11. **Answer (A) is correct.** In *Pap's A.M. v. City of Erie*, 529 U.S. 277 (2000), the Court upheld such a restriction, with members of the Court either using a secondary effects or a public morality rationale for upholding the ban.

Answer (B) is incorrect because in *Pap's* there was not a majority for the proposition that the nude component of dancing was itself content, and thus not a majority for the proposition that a ban on nude dancing was content-based.

Answer (C) is incorrect because a majority in *Pap's* considered dancing to be expression. *See also Ward v. Rock Against Racism*, 491 U.S. 781 (1989) (music is speech).

Answer (D) is incorrect because a majority of the Court in *Pap's* rejected the proposition that nude dancing was a particular category of expression, in favor of an approach in which erotic dancing was the appropriate category; because the ordinance allowed erotic dancing with minimal clothing, some avenue for that expression remained.

5.12.   **Answer (D) is correct.** This case is governed by the symbolic speech doctrine of *United States v. O'Brien*, 391 U.S. 367 (1968). In *O'Brien*, the Court allowed the government to punish expressive conduct if it had a legitimate reason to ban the conduct, unrelated to the expression that conduct carried with it, and if there was no other reasonable way for government to further that interest. That test is expressed by Answer (D).

Answer (A) is incorrect because *O'Brien* allowed the government to punish conduct even if it was intended as expression.

Answer (B) is incorrect because under *O'Brien* the First Amendment does give some degree of protection to such expressive conduct.

Answer (C) is incorrect because the sincerity of the speaker's desire to express himself has no bearing on whether government can punish expressive conduct. *See O'Brien.*

5.13.   **Answer (D) is correct** because the Court has not held that vague laws are invalid in every area of the law. *See Grayned v. City of Rockford*, 408 U.S. 104 (1972).

Answer (A) is incorrect because the Court has stated that vague laws are objectionable in part because they fail to give adequate notice to those subject to the law, and accordingly fail to give them an opportunity to comply with the law. *See Grayned v. City of Rockford, supra.*

Answer (B) is incorrect because the Court has stated that vague laws are objectionable because they vest arbitrary and discriminatory enforcement power in administrators. *See Grayned v. City of Rockford, supra.*

Answer (C) is incorrect because the Court has stated that the vagueness doctrine has special force as applied to laws affecting free speech. *See Grayned v. City of Rockford, supra.*

5.14.   **Answer (B) is correct** because the Court's rules do not absolutely preclude "facial" challenges, and therefore this is the one reason that the Court would not give for disfavoring "as applied" challenges. *See New York v. Ferber*, 458 U.S. 747 (1982).

Answer (A) is incorrect because the Court disfavors "facial" challenges because it wishes to focus on the facts before the Court — the law "as applied" to the plaintiff — rather than on abstract principles. *Id.*

Answer (C) is incorrect because, as a general rule, litigants are not allowed to raise the rights of others not before the Court. *Id.*

Answer (D) is incorrect because it states a valid reason for requiring "as applied" challenges. *Id. See also* the discussion of Answer (A), above.

5.15.   **Answer (C) is correct.** In general, the Court requires "substantial overbreadth" before it will strike down an overbroad law. *See New York v. Ferber*, 458 U.S. 747 (1982). As a result, Answer (C), which refers to "substantial overbreadth," is the correct answer.

Answer (A) is incorrect because it refers to "some" overbreadth while substantial overbreadth is required. *Id.*

Answer (B) is incorrect because it refers to "any" overbreadth while the Court requires "substantial overbreadth." *Id.*

Answer (D) is incorrect because the Court does not require "great" overbreadth. *Id.*

5.16. In *Connally v. General Construction Co.*, 269 U.S. 385, 391 (1926), the Court said that "a statute which either forbids or requires the doing of an act in terms so vague that men of common intelligence must necessarily guess at its meaning and differ as to its application violates the first essential of due process of law." There are two justifications for the vagueness doctrine: "First, [vague laws] may trap the innocent by not providing fair warning. Second, if arbitrary and discriminatory enforcement is to be prevented, laws must provide explicit standards for those who apply them. A vague law impermissibly delegates basic policy matters to policemen, judges, and juries for resolution on an ad hoc and subjective basis, with the attendant dangers of arbitrary and discriminatory application." *Grayned v. City of Rockford*, 408 U.S. 104 (1972).

5.17. A "prior restraint" is a restriction or prohibition on the circulation of ideas that occurs prior to the dissemination of those ideas. In English common law, prior restraints were common and included such restrictions as licensing. In this country, as the Court recognized in *Bantam Books, Inc. v. Sullivan*, 372 U.S. 58, 70 (1962): "Any system of prior restraints of expression comes to this Court bearing a heavy presumption against its constitutional validity." Prior restraints are particularly objectionable because they prevent ideas from reaching the public.

5.18. The classical form of a prior restraint arose in England several hundred years ago. With the invention of the printing press, people could communicate ideas more effectively and more widely. Previously, people had been able to communicate information only by word of mouth or handwritten documents. By these methods, information could be widely disseminated, but the process required time and a great deal of effort. Because the printing press allowed ideas to be more easily circulated, it was regarded as more threatening and more dangerous. Accordingly, the English Crown imposed licensing schemes that required the press to submit manuscripts to government censors prior to publication. A license could be denied, or it could be granted on condition that certain objectionable information be deleted.

5.19. **Answer (C) is correct.** In *Lovell v. City of Griffin*, 303 U.S. 444 (1938), the Court held (in accord with Answer (C)) that the ordinance was invalid on its face as an unconstitutional prior restraint.

Answer (A) is incorrect because *Lovell* did not hold that the ordinance was constitutional; in general, states do not have a valid interest in controlling the distribution of literature.

Answer (B) is incorrect because *Lovell* did not hold that the ordinance was constitutional because it was narrowly tailored.

Answer (D) is incorrect because *Lovell* did not invoke this balancing test.

5.20. **Answer (D) is correct** because *Lovell* did not hold that freedom of the press extends to newspapers, but not to pamphlets and circulars.

Answer (A) is incorrect because *Lovell* held that the Griffin, Georgia ordinance involved an example of censorship and licensing in its baldest form.

Answer (B) is incorrect because *Lovell* held that the ordinance strikes at the very foundation of freedom of the press by subjecting literature and circulars to censorship.

Answer (C) is incorrect because *Lovell* held that freedom of the press is not limited to newspapers, but extends to pamphlets and circulars.

5.21. **Answer (B) is correct** because the court does uphold content-neutral time, place, and manner restrictions on speech. *See Cox v. New Hampshire*, 312 U.S. 569 (1941).

Answer (A) is incorrect because the Court has not held that all licensing restraints on speech are necessarily invalid. *See Cox v. New Hampshire.*

Answer (C) is incorrect because, as Answer (B) indicates, the Court upholds licensing schemes when they involve content-neutral time, place and manner restrictions, which generally do not require support by a compelling government interest. *See Cox v. New Hampshire.*

Answer (D) is incorrect because the Court does not hold that licensing restrictions are exempt from prior restraint constraints. *Id.*

5.22. **Answer (D) is correct** because in *Freedman* all of these conditions were identified as necessary for a valid film licensing scheme.

Answer (A) is incorrect because *Freedman* held that all of these conditions were necessary for a motion picture licensing scheme to be valid.

Answer (B) is incorrect because *Freedman* held that all of these conditions were necessary for a motion picture licensing scheme to be valid.

Answer (C) is incorrect because *Freedman* held that all of these conditions were necessary for a motion picture licensing scheme to be valid.

5.23. **Answer (C) is correct** because in *Bantam Books, Inc. v. Sullivan*, 372 U.S. 58 (1963), the Court held that governmental censors were not free to notify distributors that certain designated books or magazines distributed by them had been reviewed and had been declared by a majority of its members to be objectionable for sale, distribution, or display to youths under 18 years of age. In so holding, the Court stated that:

> [It] would be naive to credit the State's assertion that these blacklists are in the nature of mere legal advice, when they plainly serve as instruments of regulation independent of the laws against obscenity. [What] Rhode Island has done [has] been to subject the distribution of publications to a

system of prior administrative restraints, since the Commission is not a judicial body and its decisions to list particular publications as objectionable do not follow judicial determinations that such publications may lawfully be banned. Any system of prior restraints of expression comes to this Court bearing a heavy presumption against its constitutional validity. We have tolerated such a system only where it operated under judicial superintendence and assured an almost immediate judicial determination of the validity of the restraint. The system at bar includes no such saving features. . . .

Answer (A) is incorrect because in *Bantam Books*, the Court made clear that the bookseller was under a *de facto* legal obligation to not sell the books on the list.

Answer (B) is incorrect because, in *Bantam Books* the Court expressed concern about the lack of procedural safeguards in its system of dealing with booksellers, independent of any state interest in protecting its youth.

Answer (D) is incorrect because in *Bantam Books* the Court found "nave" the idea that there was no state compulsion, and thus no state action, in its circulation to booksellers of lists of objectionable books.

5.24. **Answer (B) is correct** because *Kingsley* held that the denial was unconstitutional because it improperly censored an idea (the notion that adultery is a "desirable, acceptable, and proper" form of behavior).

Answer (A) is incorrect because *Kingsley* did not hold that the denial was proper.

Answer (C) is incorrect because *Kingsley* did not hold that under its police power, the state has the right to prohibit dangerous ideas relating to such things as adultery.

Answer (D) is incorrect because *Kingsley* did not hold that adultery is an unprotected idea.

5.25. **Answer (D) is correct** In *Near*, the Court held that the injunction constituted an invalid prior restraint, which is presumptively unconstitutional.

Answer (A) is incorrect because *Near* did not hold that, even though prior restraints are disfavored, injunctions against newspapers that publish "malicious, scandalous, and defamatory" material are permissible. Rather, *Near* noted the availability of post-publication legal remedies for such conduct.

Answer (B) is incorrect because *Near* did not hold that an injunction against a newspaper is permissible if issued by a court rather than by an administrative official.

Answer (C) is incorrect because *Near* did not hold that injunctions against newspapers are permissible when the newspaper is being operated as a "public nuisance."

5.26. *New York Times Co. v. United States*, 403 U.S. 713 (1971), also known as the "Pentagon Papers" case, involved the United States government's attempt to enjoin a newspaper from publishing classified documents involving United States participation in the Vietnam War. In both cases the district courts refused to issue injunctions. On appeal, the government prevailed in the Second Circuit (the *New York Times* case), but lost in the District of Columbia (the *Washington Post* case). The Court rendered the following ruling:

> We granted certiorari in these cases in which the United States seeks to enjoin the New York Times and the Washington Post from publishing the contents of a classified study entitled "History of U.S. Decision-Making Process on Viet Nam Policy."

> "Any system of prior restraints of expression comes to this Court bearing a heavy presumption against its constitutional validity." *Bantam Books, Inc. v. Sullivan*, 372 U.S. 58, 70 (1963); *see also Near v. Minnesota ex rel. Olson*, 283 U.S. 697 (1931). The Government "thus carries a heavy burden of showing justification for the imposition of such a restraint." The District Court for the Southern District of New York in the New York Times case, and the District Court for the District of Columbia and the Court of Appeals for the District of Columbia Circuit in the Washington Post case held that the Government had not met that burden. We agree.

Thus, in essence, the Court recognized that prior restraints carry a heavy presumption of unconstitutionality, which the government did not rebut.

5.27. **Answer (B) is correct.** In *Madsen*, the Court held that it must ask whether the challenged provisions of the injunction burden no more speech than necessary to serve a significant government interest.

Answer (A) is incorrect because *Madsen* did not hold that injunctions, like other prior restraints, should be subject to strict scrutiny.

Answer (C) is incorrect because *Madsen* did not hold that injunctions, since they are issued by judges, are subject to only rational basis review; the review was more stringent than mere rational basis review.

Answer (D) is incorrect because *Madsen* did not hold that injunctions against abortion protestors should be treated as content-based and viewpoint-based restrictions on speech.

5.28. **Answer (C) is correct** because *Madsen v. Women's Health Center, Inc.*, 512 U.S. 753 (1994), held that the mere fact that the injunction covered people with a particular viewpoint did not itself render the injunction content or viewpoint-based. The Court stated:

> Here, the state court imposed restrictions on [the protesters] incidental to their antiabortion message because they repeatedly violated the court's original order. That [the protesters] all share the same viewpoint regarding abortion does not in itself demonstrate that some invidious content- or viewpoint-based purpose motivated the issuance of the order. It suggests only that those in the group whose conduct violated the court's order happen to share the same opinion regarding abortions being performed at the clinic.

In short, the fact that the injunction covered people with a particular viewpoint does not itself render the injunction content or viewpoint based. Accordingly, the injunction issued in this case does not demand [a] level of heightened [scrutiny].

Answer (A) is incorrect because *Madsen* did not hold that the injunction constituted a content-based restriction on the abortion protestor's speech.

Answer (B) is incorrect because *Madsen* did not hold that the injunction constituted a viewpoint-based restriction on speech.

Answer (D) is incorrect because *Madsen* did not hold that the injunction constituted both a content-based and a viewpoint-based restriction on speech; indeed, it found that it was neither.

5.29. **Answer (B) is correct** because *United States v. O'Brien*, 391 U.S. 367 (1968), required that government restrictions on expressive conduct not be motivated by a desire to suppress that expression.

Answer (A) is incorrect because the Court has made it clear that expressive conduct (*e.g.*, burning a draft card in order to express opposition to a military draft) has some First Amendment protection. *See United States v. O'Brien*.

Answer (C) is incorrect because, as in *O'Brien* itself, the Court has allowed the government to penalize conduct that has an expressive element, as long as the appropriate test is satisfied.

Answer (D) is incorrect because the appropriate test, from *O'Brien*, requires more than a rational basis. In particular, *O'Brien* requires, among other things, that the government restriction be no more speech-restrictive than necessary to accomplish the government's legitimate, non-expression-supressive objective in penalizing the conduct. This standard reflects a tougher test than mere rational basis.

6.1.   Some have argued that the press clause grants the press special privileges not available under the free speech clause. For example, Justice Powell, concurring in *Branzburg v. Hayes*, 408 U.S. 665 (1972), stated that: "The press has a preferred position in our constitutional scheme, not to enable it to make money, not to set newsmen apart as a favored class, but to bring fulfillment to the public's right to know. The right to know is crucial to the governing powers of the people. . . . Knowledge is essential to informed decisions." Others disagree. For example, then Chief Justice Burger, concurring in *First National Bank of Boston v. Bellotti*, 435 U.S. 765 (1978), stated that:

> [The] Court has not yet squarely resolved whether the Press Clause confers upon the "institutional press" any freedom from government restraint not enjoyed by all others. [A]lthough certainty on this point is not possible, the history of the Clause does not suggest that the authors contemplated a "special" or "institutional" privilege. The common 18th century understanding of freedom of the press is suggested by Andrew Bradford, a colonial American newspaperman. In defining the nature of the liberty, he did not limit it to a particular group:

> "[By] Freedom of the Press, I mean a Liberty, within the Bounds of Law, for any Man to communicate to the Public, his Sentiments on the Important Points of Religion and Government; of proposing any Laws, which he apprehends may be for the Good of his Countrey, and of applying for the Repeal of such, as he Judges pernicious. . . .

> "This is the Liberty of the Press, the great Palladium of all our other Liberties. . . ."

A. Bradford, *Sentiments on the Liberty of the Press*, in L. LEVY, FREEDOM OF THE PRESS FROM ZENGER TO JEFFERSON 41–42 (1966) (first published in Bradford's *The American Weekly Mercury*, a Philadelphia newspaper, Apr. 25, 1734).

There is no precise answer or resolution to these disparate views of the press. One commentator indicated that most pre-First Amendment commentators "who employed the term 'freedom of speech' with great frequency, used it synonomously with freedom of the press." L. LEVY, LEGACY OF SUPPRESSION: FREEDOM OF SPEECH AND PRESS IN EARLY AMERICAN HISTORY 174 (1960).

6.2.   **Answer (C) is correct.** In *Branzburg v. Hayes*, 408 U.S. 665 (1972), the Court rejected the reporter's refusal to testify and his First Amendment defense. The Court held that the public interest in gathering information about crime outweighed the reporter's interest in withholding the testimony.

Answer (A) is incorrect because *Branzburg* did not accept the reporter's refusal and did not suggest that the First Amendment gives reporters an absolute right to refuse to reveal their sources. Indeed, the Court rejected the reporter's claim to immunity from testifying in that particular case.

Answer (B) is incorrect because *Branzburg* did not accept the reporter's refusal and did not hold that a refusal to recognize a reporter's First Amendment privilege would undermine the freedom of the press to collect and disseminate news. Indeed, the Court noted that a reporter's privilege had been presumed not to exist for most of American history, yet the press had flourished.

Answer (D) is incorrect because *Branzburg* did not hold that reporters are not protected under the First Amendment. In particular, Justice Powell's fifth-vote concurring opinion makes clear that the First Amendment does protect reporters from misuse of the subpoena process.

6.3.   **Answer (B) is correct.** *Cohen* held that:

> [G]enerally applicable laws do not offend the First Amendment simply because their enforcement against the press has incidental effects on its ability to gather and report the news. [The] press may not with impunity break and enter an office or dwelling to gather news. Neither does the First Amendment relieve a newspaper reporter of the obligation shared by all citizens to respond to a grand jury subpoena. . . .

> [The reporter and his employer] argue that permitting [the source] to maintain a cause of action for promissory estoppel will inhibit truthful reporting because news organizations will have legal incentives not to disclose a confidential source's identity even when that person's identity is itself newsworthy. [I]f this is the case, it is no more than the incidental, and constitutionally insignificant, consequence of applying to the press a generally applicable law that requires those who make certain kinds of promises to keep them. . . .

Answer (A) is incorrect because *Cohen* did not hold that the First Amendment prevents a reporter from being sued for breaching a promise of confidentiality to a source.

Answer (C) is incorrect because *Cohen* did not hold that the First Amendment prevents a reporter from being sued for breaching a promise of confidentiality to a source absent a showing of "actual malice" in the reporter's decision to breach. Reporters are subject to general contract rules without any special protections.

Answer (D) is incorrect because *Cohen* did not hold that the First Amendment exempts reporters from general contract law. Indeed, it held the opposite.

6.4.   **Answer (A) is correct.** In *Zurcher* the Court upheld the search warrant and the search finding no violation of either the First or Fourteenth Amendments to the United States Constitution. The Court concluded that the First Amendment (as incorporated through the Fourteenth) does not prohibit the issuance of warrants permitting searches of newspaper offices.

Answer (B) is incorrect because *Zurcher* did not hold that the First Amendment absolutely prohibits the police from obtaining search warrants authorizing intrusion into newspaper offices.

Answer (C) is incorrect because *Zurcher* did not hold that the First Amendment prohibits the police from obtaining search warrants.

Answer (D) is incorrect because *Zurcher* did not impose an appellate review requirement for all search warrants aimed at newspaper offices.

6.5.   **Answer (B) is correct** because in *Globe Newspaper*, the Court held that a case-by-case closure process was a more narrowly-tailored way of promoting the state's interest in protecting young victims from the adverse effects of having to testify in public about the crimes against them.

Answer (A) is incorrect because *Globe* did not conclude that a mandatory closure law was necessary to protect young victims.

Answer (C) is incorrect because *Globe* did not adopt such a blanket rule. Instead, it required case-by-case judgments striking this balance.

Answer (D) is incorrect because the Court did not hold that the press has no right of access to judicial proceedings.

6.6.   In *Globe Newspaper Co.* the Court placed particular reliance on the fact that criminal trials have historically been open to the press and the general public, and that the right of access to criminal trials plays a particularly significant role in the functioning of the judicial process and the government as a whole. Thus, history, and what the Court called "the favorable judgment of experience," counseled in favor of openness.

6.7.   **Answer (C) is correct** because *Press-Enterprise* held that the First Amendment gives the press and the public a right of access. Confidence in the system requires transparency. Such access can only be denied if there is a "substantial probability" of prejudice to the defendant's right to a fair trial, and that risk cannot be mitigated by less stringent limits on First Amendment rights.

Answer (A) is incorrect because *Press-Enterprise* insisted on more than a "reasonable necessity" before a preliminary hearing could be closed and the transcript sealed.

Answer (B) is incorrect because *Press-Enterprise* did not hold that the judge acted correctly in closing the hearing.

Answer (D) is incorrect because *Press-Enterprise* did not hold that the press has no right of access to transcripts.

6.8.   **Answer (C) is correct.** In *Chandler*, the Court held that television cameras in a trial courtroom is not inherently a denial of due process, and concluded that the defendant had not shown that, in his particular case, the presence of cameras violated due process.

Answer (A) is incorrect because *Chandler* did not hold that a trial court may not allow radio, television, and still photographic coverage of a trial over the accused's objections. Indeed, the Court allowed cameras in that case, despite the defendant's objections.

Answer (B) is incorrect because *Chandler* did not hold that a trial court has free rein to permit radio, television, and still photographic coverage without regard to an accused's objections. Indeed, the Court considered whether such coverage made the defendant's trial unfair.

Answer (D) is incorrect because *Chandler* did not hold that radio and television reporters must be excluded from all judicial proceedings. In fact, the Court allowed cameras in that case.

6.9.   **Answer (A) is correct** because *Pell* held that the press does not have a constitutional right of special access to information not available to the public generally.

     Answer (B) is incorrect because *Pell* did not hold that inmates, like other citizens, have a First Amendment right to free speech which includes the right to do interviews with the media.

     Answer (C) is incorrect because *Pell* did not hold that the media has a First Amendment right to interview prison inmates. Indeed, they upheld the prison's refusal of such interview opportunities.

     Answer (D) is incorrect because *Pell* did not hold that the First Amendment has no application in the prison context. The Court did not rule so broadly.

6.10.   **Answer (B) is correct** because *Sheppard* held that, since the state trial judge did not fulfill his duty to protect Sheppard from the inherently prejudicial publicity that saturated the community, the defendant did not receive a fair trial and thus the habeas writ should have been granted.

     Answer (A) is incorrect because *Sheppard* did not hold that defendant received a fair trial.

     Answer (C) is incorrect because *Sheppard* did not hold that the trial court should have entered a gag order prohibiting all pretrial publicity. Indeed, such orders are strongly disfavored.

     Answer (D) is incorrect because *Sheppard* focused on the fairness of the trial, not on the abstract right of a defendant to a trial with restricted publicity. Moreover, the Court in *Sheppard* granted the petition.

6.11.   In *Nebraska Press Association v. Stuart*, 427 U.S. 539 (1976), the Court suggested that a trial court might take any of the following actions to minimize the adverse effects of heavy publicity on a criminal defendant's fair trial right:

> Most of the alternatives to prior restraint of publication in these circumstances [*i.e.*, a gag order] were discussed with obvious approval in *Sheppard v. Maxwell*: (a) change of trial venue to a place less exposed to the

intense publicity . . . ; (b) postponement of the trial to allow public attention to subside; (c) searching questioning of prospective jurors . . . to screen out those with fixed opinions as to guilt or innocence; (d) the use of emphatic and clear instructions on the sworn duty of each juror to decide the issues only on evidence presented in open court. Sequestration of jurors is, of course, always available. Although that measure insulates jurors only after they are sworn, it also enhances the likelihood of dissipating the impact of pretrial publicity and emphasizes the elements of the jurors' [oaths].

TOPIC 7:   ANSWERS

BROADCAST REGULATION & OTHER "ADVANCING" FORMS OF TECHNOLOGY

7.1.   **Answer (B) is correct** because *Red Lion* held that the broadcast media deserves less First Amendment protection than books and newspapers, given the fact that scarce broadcast spectrum space makes that medium more amenable to regulation.

Answer (A) is incorrect because *Red Lion* did not hold that the broadcast media should be treated like newspapers and books in that it receives broad First Amendment protections. Indeed, *Red Lion* upheld restrictions on broadcast speakers that would probably be unconstitutional if applied to newspapers and books. *See, e.g., Miami Herald v. Tornillo*, 418 U.S. 241 (1974) (striking down right-of-reply statute aimed at newspapers even though analogous "fairness doctrine" regulation was upheld in *Red Lion* as applied to broadcasters).

Answer (C) is incorrect because *Red Lion* did not hold that the broadcast media is deserving of no First Amendment protection whatsoever.

Answer (D) is incorrect because *Red Lion* did not hold that the broadcast medium deserves more First Amendment protection than books and newspapers.

7.2.   In *Red Lion*, the Court offered a number of justifications for treating the broadcast media differently for First Amendment purposes. These included the fact that there is a limited amount of broadcast spectrum space, and not everyone can communicate at once. The Court stated: "The lack of know-how and equipment may keep many from the air, but only a tiny fraction of those with resources and intelligence can hope to communicate by radio at the same time if intelligible communication is to be had, even if the entire radio spectrum is utilized in the present state of commercially acceptable technology." Since such a small number of frequencies are available, and the government allocates those frequencies to a small number of individuals, the government has the right to limit how those frequencies are used.

The Court continued:

> By the same token, as far as the First Amendment is concerned those who are licensed stand no better than those to whom licenses are refused. A license permits broadcasting, but the licensee has no constitutional right to be the one who holds the license or to monopolize a radio frequency to the exclusion of his fellow citizens. There is nothing in the First Amendment which prevents the Government from requiring a licensee to share his frequency with others and to conduct himself as a proxy or fiduciary with obligations to present those views and voices which are representative of his community and which would otherwise, by necessity, be barred from the

airwaves.

7.3.   **Answer (C) is correct.** In *Red Lion*, the Court upheld the "fairness doctrine," holding that it was consistent with the more limited protections provided to broadcasters.

Answer (A) is incorrect because *Red Lion* did not consider the "multiple ownership" rule.

Answer (B) is incorrect because *Red Lion* did not consider the "After 10:00 p.m." rule.

Answer (D) is incorrect because *Red Lion* did not consider the "Children's Programming" rule.

7.4.   **Answer (B) is correct** because *Pacifica Foundation* placed great weight on the invasive nature of broadcast media, and concluded that content inappropriate for children could be "channeled" to times of the day when children were less likely to be listening.

Answer (A) is incorrect because *Pacifica Foundation* did not hold that content such as the "Filthy Words" monologue could be banned from the airwaves. Instead, the Court emphasized that its holding was narrow, confined only to the administrative order against broadcasting the program during daytime hours.

Answer (C) is incorrect because *Pacifica Foundation* did not hold that the radio station has an absolute right to air all programs; instead, the Court upheld the FCC's order against the broadcaster.

Answer (D) is incorrect because *Pacifica Foundation* concluded that the intrusive nature of radio and the inability to constantly broadcast warnings about mature content made simply tuning to another station an inadequate protection from undesired profanity.

7.5.   **Answer (B) is correct.** In *Turner I* the Court suggested that the government might have the power to impose the "must carry" rules. However, the Court remanded for further hearings. In *Turner II* the Court upheld the "must carry" rules based on findings made by the lower court on remand in *Turner I*.

Answer (A) is incorrect because the *Turner Broadcasting* cases upheld congressional mandates on what channels cable companies must carry on their systems.

Answer (C) is incorrect because *Turner Broadcasting* did not hold the "must carry" rule constitutes a "taking" that requires compensation.

Answer (D) is incorrect because *Turner Broadcasting* did not hold that cable companies have a constitutional right to exclude local stations.

7.6.   **Answer (A) is correct** because in *Denver Area*, the Court upheld § 10(a).

Answer (B) is incorrect because *Denver Area* struck down § 10(c).

Answer (C) is incorrect because *Denver Area* struck down the remaining provision (which required cable system operators to segregate certain "patently offensive" programming, to place it on a single channel, and to block that channel from viewer access unless the viewer requests access in advance and in writing).

Answer (D) is incorrect because *Denver Area* the Court did not uphold both of these provisions, only the first.

7.7.   **Answer (C) is correct** because in *Reno*, the Court held that Internet speech did not possess the characteristics of broadcast media that justified lesser scrutiny of speech restrictions in *Red Lion Broadcasting v. FCC*, 395 U.S. 367 (1969) and *FCC v. Pacifica Foundation*, 438 U.S. 726 (1978).

Answer (A) is incorrect because the Court rejected applying to the Internet the lower level of scrutiny accorded broadcasting, since the Internet does not suffer the same scarcity concerns justifying lesser protection for broadcasting.

Answer (B) is incorrect because *Reno* rejected this argument, describing it as "singularly unpersuasive" given the rapid rise in Internet usage before enactment of the statute.

Answer (D) is incorrect because in *Reno*, the Court applied much more than intermediate scrutiny to Internet speech. *See Reno* ("The breadth of [the statute's] content-based restriction on speech imposes an especially heavy burden on the Government to explain why a less restrictive provision would not be as effective as [the statute].").

7.8.   In *Reno v. American Civil Liberties Union*, 521 U.S. 844 (1997), the Court suggested that the Internet is fundamentally different than broadcast regulation. Unlike the broadcast media, which has a limited number of frequencies and therefore cannot be freely available to everyone, the Internet is easily and cheaply accessible. Moreover, there is less likelihood of encountering content by accident, as compared with radio broadcasting. As a result, the Court concluded that the Internet should be treated differently than the broadcast media.

7.9.   **Answer is (D) is correct** because it states the result and reasoning in *Ashcroft v. ACLU*, 542 U.S. 656 (2004), which dealt with an analogous statute.

Answer (A) is incorrect because it has been the case since *Reno v. ACLU*, 521 U.S. 844 (1997), that speech on the Internet enjoys full First Amendment protection.

Answer (B) is incorrect because speech that is harmful to minors retains full First Amendment protection with regard to access by adults, unless it is child pornography (which the material regulated here is not).

Answer (C) is incorrect because it places the burden of proof on the wrong party. *Ashcroft* reaffirmed the rule that government has the burden of proof with regard to content-based regulations. Here, it is government that must prove that filters are *not* effective — not, as Answer (C) states, the plaintiffs who must prove that filters *are* effective.

7.10.   **Answer (D) is correct** because the Court has not held that, based on history or any other consideration, the broadcast medium is not entitled to constitutional protection. *See FCC v. Pacifica Foundation*, 428 U.S. 726 (1978).

Answer (A) is incorrect because the Court considers the pervasiveness of the medium subject to regulation as a relevant consideration. *See Pacifica.*

Answer (B) is incorrect because the Court considers the ease with which children could access that medium unsupervised by adults as a relevant consideration. *Pacifica; see also Sable Communications v. FCC*, 492 U.S. 115 (1989) (noting that "dial-a-porn" services are not easily accessible to children).

Answer (C) is incorrect because in *Reno v. ACLU*, 521 U.S. 844 (1997), the Court cited the communicative potential of the Internet in striking down federal regulation of indecent speech in that medium.

8.1.   **Answer (A) is correct** because *NAACP* noted, when recognizing a right of association, that "[e]ffective advocacy of both public and private points of view, particularly controversial ones, is undeniably enhanced by group association."

Answer (B) is incorrect because the right to freedom of association is not explicitly articulated in the Fifth Amendment.

Answer (C) is incorrect because the right to freedom of association is not explicitly articulated in the First Amendment.

Answer (D) is incorrect because the right to freedom of association is not explicitly articulated in the Ninth Amendment.

8.2.   **Answer (B) is correct.** In *NAACP*, the Court held that the right to freedom of association protected the NAACP against disclosure of its membership lists. If the lists were disclosed, the NAACP's members risked retaliation because of their membership.

Answer (A) is incorrect because in its decision in *NAACP*, the Court weighed, as part of its First Amendment analysis, the risk that private parties might harm the group's members if the group had to disclose its membership list.

Answer (C) is incorrect because *NAACP* protected the confidentiality of the membership list on a freedom of association ground.

Answer (D) is incorrect because *NAACP* did not hold that the right to freedom of association is inapplicable to corporations and entities like the NAACP.

8.3.   In *Barnette*, the Court stated that to "sustain the compulsory flag salute we are required to say that a Bill of Rights which guards the individual's right to speak his own mind, left it open to public authorities to compel him to utter what is not in his mind." The Court went on to state that, if "there is any fixed star in our constitutional constellation, it is that no official, high or petty, can prescribe what shall be orthodox in politics, nationalism, religion, or other matters of opinion or force citizens to confess by word or act their faith therein." It thus struck down the mandatory flag salute statute because it violated the First Amendment for government to compel speech just as it violated the First Amendment for government to prohibit it.

8.4.   **Answer (B) is correct.** In *Hurley* the Court held that parade organizers had a First Amendment right to disassociate themselves from GLIB's message. In creating the parade, the organizers were articulating a message and they were permitted to limit that message in the way they chose.

Answer (A) is incorrect because *Hurley* did not hold GLIB had a free speech right to participate in the St. Patrick's Day parade.

Answer (C) is incorrect because *Hurley* did not hold that the right to Freedom of Association is inapplicable to parades. Indeed, it held the opposite when ruled in favor of the organizers.

Answer (D) is incorrect because *Hurley* held that application of the public accommodation law to GLIB's demand to be included in the parade would violate the parade organizers' First Amendment rights.

8.5.   **Answer (C) is correct.** In *Dale,* the Court held that the Boy Scouts' claim of freedom of association prevailed over Dale's claim under the New Jersey law. In other words, New Jersey could not force the Boy Scouts to admit someone whose identity was inconsistent with their message.

Answer (A) is incorrect because *Dale* did not hold that the New Jersey public accommodations law trumps the Boy Scouts' right to freedom of association. Indeed, it held the opposite.

Answer (B) is incorrect because *Dale* held that vindication of Dale's right under the state law would violate the Scouts' constitutional rights.

Answer (D) is incorrect because *Dale* did not hold that discrimination against gays and lesbians is impermissible under the Constitution. The only discrimination at issue was performed by a private party (the Boy Scouts); thus there was no occasion for the Court to consider a claim of unconstitutional discrimination against gays and lesbians.

8.6.   **Answer (D) is correct** because it is an inaccurate statement of *Southworth's* analysis. In *Southworth,* the Court held that student activity fees are subject to First Amendment protections; it just held that in this particular case there was no First Amendment violation.

Answer (A) is incorrect because *Southworth* assumed that the students had First Amendment rights in this context, even if they voluntarily chose to attend the university.

Answer (B) is incorrect because *Southworth* did hold that the University must provide some protection to its students' First Amendment interests.

Answer (C) is incorrect because *Southworth* did hold that students are entitled to protections designed to ensure that the program is administered in a viewpoint-neutral manner.

PART II
THE RELIGION CLAUSES

ANSWERS

TOPIC 9:   ANSWERS
THE ESTABLISHMENT CLAUSE

9.1.   **Answer (D) is correct.** By its explicit terms, the Establishment Clause applies only to Congress.

Answer (A) is incorrect. By its explicit terms, the Establishment Clause does not apply to all levels of governments (federal, state, and local). Indeed, the First Amendment refers only to Congress.

Answer (B) is incorrect. By its explicit terms, the Establishment Clause does not apply only to the states. Indeed, the First Amendment refers only to Congress.

Answer (C) is incorrect. By its explicit terms, the Establishment Clause does not apply to the entire federal government. The First Amendment refers to Congress.

9.2.   **Answer (A) is correct.** The United States Supreme Court has interpreted and applied the Establishment Clause to all levels of government in the United States (federal, state, and local). The Clause applies to state and local governments through its "incorporation" via the Due Process Clause of the Fourteenth Amendment.

Answer (B) is incorrect. As interpreted and applied by the courts today, the Establishment Clause has not been interpreted as applying only to the states. Indeed, by its explicit terms the Clause applies to Congress. As noted, the United States Supreme Court has interpreted and applied the Establishment Clause to all levels of government in the United States (federal, state, and local).

Answer (C) is incorrect. As interpreted and applied by the courts today, the Establishment Clause has not been been applied only to the Federal government. As noted, the United States Supreme Court has interpreted and applied the Establishment Clause to all levels of government in the United States (federal, state, and local). The Clause applies to state and local governments through its "incorporation" via the Due Process Clause of the Fourteenth Amendment.

Answer (D) is incorrect. As interpreted and applied by the courts today, the Establishment Clause has not been applied to Congress only. As noted, the United States Supreme Court has interpreted and applied the Establishment Clause to all levels of government in the United States (federal, state, and local). The Clause applies to state and local governments through its "incorporation" via the Due Process Clause of the Fourteenth Amendment. It has also been interpreted to apply to all branches of the federal government, not just Congress, despite its seemingly clear language limiting only Congress.

9.3.   **Answer (D) is correct.** The Establishment Clause has been interpreted as applying to a variety of governmental actions beyond just the declaration of an "official" religion. In addition to applying to situations when the government attempts to require mandatory church attendance, or profession of belief or disbelief in a particular religion, the Clause has also been applied, for example, to government funding of religious institutions. *See, e.g., Committee v. Public Education v. Nyquist*, 413 U.S. 756 (1973) (striking down government aid to religious schools).

Answer (A) is incorrect. It is not accurate to state that the Establishment Clause has been interpreted as *only* prohibiting governments from declaring an "official" religion.

Answer (B) is incorrect. It is not accurate to state that the Establishment Clause has been interpreted as *only* prohibiting governments from requiring mandatory church attendance.

Answer (C) is incorrect. It is not accurate to state that the Establishment Clause has been interpreted as *only* in these situations. See the explanation to answer (D), above.

9.4.   **Answer (A) correct** because the Establishment Clause has not been applied to prohibit private (individual) prayer in public settings.

Answer (B) is incorrect because the Establishment Clause has been applied in some contexts to prohibit government-provided financial aid to religious organizations, *See, e.g., Committee v. Public Education v. Nyquist*, 413 U.S. 756 (1973).

Answer (C) is incorrect because the Establishment Clause has been applied to prohibit official prayers in public schools. *See, e.g., Engel v. Vitale*, 370 U.S. 421 (1962).

Answer (D) is incorrect because the Establishment Clause has been applied to prohibit government-sponsored Christmas displays. *See, e.g., Allegheny County v. ACLU*, 492 U.S. 573 (1989).

9.5.   **Answer (A) is correct** because it reflects the resolution of a similar issue in *Allegheny County v. ACLU*, 492 U.S. 573 (1989). In that case, four justices would have allowed a nativity scene based on a community's right to acknowledge holidays with both cultural and religious aspects, while two other justices held that a combination of secular and religious symbols of a given holiday was constitutional because it did not have the effect of endorsing religion.

Answer (B) is incorrect because it reflects too broad a view of the Establishment Clause as understood by the Court, since it would prohibit any display that might have a religious message, such as a religious painting hung in a government-run museum.

Answer (C) is incorrect because its approach did not capture majority support in *Allegheny County*. See the explanation to answer (A), above.

Answer (D) is incorrect because the Establishment Clause can be violated by government actions short of compelling worship. *See, e.g., Allegheny County.*

9.6.   **Answer (B) is correct** because it correctly states the first rule from *Lemon v. Kurtzman*, 403 U.S. 602 (1971), which remains the general rule for Establishment Clause challenges.

Answer (A) is incorrect because *Lemon* requires, among other things, that the government action not have the primary effect of endorsing religion.

Answer (C) is incorrect because the third prong of the *Lemon* test requires that the government action not lead to an excessive entanglement between government and religion.

Answer (D) is incorrect for the same reason that answer (C) is.

9.7.   **Answer (B) is correct** because it reflects the result and reasoning in *Marsh v. Chambers*, 463 U.S. 783 (1983). In *Marsh*, the Court noted the long history of legislative chaplains, and from that history inferred that the drafters of the First Amendment did not intend for such a practice to be outlawed by the Establishment Clause.

Answer (A) is incorrect since the original Constitution does not mention the opening of congressional sessions with a prayer.

Answer (C) is incorrect because in *Marsh* the legislature had employed the same clergyman for 18 years.

Answer (D) is incorrect because *Marsh* upheld the practice of legislative chaplains.

9.8.   **Answer (C) is correct** because it reflects the analysis and result in *Walz v. Tax Commission*, 397 U.S. 664 (1970). In that case the Court noted that government had a legitimate interest in assisting such nonprofit organizations and the tax exemption did not excessively entangle the government with religion.

Answer (A) is incorrect because tax law is subject to the First Amendment, as evidenced by *Texas Monthly, Inc. v. Bullock*, 489 U.S. 1 (1989), which struck down a tax exemption given only to religious organizations.

Answer (B) is incorrect because in *Texas Monthly* the Court explained that a tax exemption given only to a religious organization conveys a message of endorsement of religion.

Answer (D) is incorrect because assistance to religion, by itself, does not violate the Establishment Clause, as made clear in cases such as *Walz*, as well as *Everson v. Board of Education*, 330 U.S. 1 (1947), which upheld government provision of buses to transport students to parochial schools.

9.9.   **Answer (C) is correct**. In *Zelman v. Simmons-Harris*, 536 U.S. 639 (2002), the Supreme Court upheld a voucher system for school students. In that case the Court noted approvingly that the aid went to parochial schools only after students and parents decided that the student would attend such schools; that is, student/parent choice broke the connection between the government money and religious organizations. When this dynamic led to most voucher money being used in parochial schools, the Supreme Court did not express a large amount of concern.

Answer (A) is incorrect because *Zelman* noted approvingly that the aid went to parochial schools only after students and parents decided that the student would attend such schools; that is, student/parent choice broke the connection between the government money and religious organizations.

Answer (B) is incorrect because *Zelman* noted approvingly that the voucher money could have been used at private but non-parochial schools.

Answer (D) is incorrect because *Zelman* noted, but did not express great concern about, the fact that the voucher amounts were closely tied to the amount of money parochial schools charged in tuition, but were lower than the amount charged by non-parochial private schools, even though this suggested that the voucher program might have a primary effect of encouraging education in religious schools.

9.10.   Probably. A similar program was upheld in *Zelman v. Simmons-Harris*, 536 U.S. 639 (2002). Under *Lemon v. Kurtzman*, 403 U.S. 602 (1971), a plan such as this alleged to violate the Establishment Clause is tested against three questions: (1) does it have a secular purpose; (2) does it have a primary effect that neither advances nor inhibits religion; and (3) does it foster an excessive government entanglement with religion? If the law either lacks a secular purpose, or has a primary effect of advancing or inhibiting religion, or fosters an excessive entanglement, it will be struck down. Here there is clearly a secular purpose — the improvement of educational opportunities for poor students. The third prong — entanglement — might be thought to be a problem, since the "no voucher money for intolerance" rule could conceivably entangle the government in making determinations about how religious doctrine is taught in religious schools. For example, the state might have to examine a religious school's religious instruction about who can enter Heaven, to determine whether that instruction teaches that non-believers are condemned to Hell. But the Court in *Zelman* held that this was not a serious problem. Finally, the second prong — the primary effect of the voucher plan — was held in *Zelman* to be satisfied because most students used their voucher money to attend non-religious schools. Thus, the primary effect of the plan was not to advance religious instruction. For these reasons, the analogous Wilson plan would probably survive.

9.11.   Probably not. Under *Lemon v. Kurtzman*, 403 U.S. 602 (1971), a statute alleged to violate the Establishment Clause is tested against three questions: (1) does it have a secular purpose; (2) does it have a primary effect that neither advances nor inhibits religion; and (3) does it foster an excessive government entanglement with religion? If the law either lacks a secular purpose, or has a primary effect of advancing or inhibiting religion, or fosters an excessive entanglement, it will be struck down. Here, it seems clear that the ordinance lacks a secular purpose. Rather, its purpose is simply to promote the creation theory of a particular religion. Moreover, its primary effect would also be to advance religion, and there might even be entanglement issues, if school officials had to decide which interpretation of Genesis (e.g., the Protestant one or the Catholic one) to present in class. For these reasons the ordinance would probably be struck down.

9.12.   Probably not. In *Lee v. Weisman*, 505 U.S. 577 (1992), the Court struck down prayers at graduation events. The majority opinion stressed the coercion implicit in the state sponsoring a prayer at an event where impressionable children may feel coerced into expressing support for a particular religion, or for religion in general. The fact that attendance at the graduation ceremony is not required did not change the analysis for the Court, which noted the importance of the ceremony to the children and their families.

9.13.   Probably not. In *Committee for Public Education v. Nyquist*, 413 U.S. 756 (1973), the Supreme Court struck down a similar law, on the ground that the effect of the aid was to provide public support for religious institutions. Thus, even though the statute may have had a secular purpose, the primary effect of the law would be to assist religious education. A different result might be reached had the law provided equivalent support for education of students in public schools. *See Zelman v. Simmons-Harris*, 536 U.S. 639 (2002) (upholding a voucher program that gave money to students to use for either public or private education). Here, though, the limitation of the reimbursement to private schools, combined with the fact that most private schools in the state were religious, would be enough to condemn the program under the Establishment Clause. It might also be relevant if the program paid money directly to the schools, as opposed to funneling it to parents/students, who would then pay the school. *See Zelman* (noting this distinction).

9.14.   Yes. In *Locke v. Davey*, 540 U.S. 712 (2004), the Supreme Court upheld an analogous program. It found no violation of the Free Exercise clause when the state was, as here, attempting to enforce a strict separation of church and state. All the state is doing is declining to fund one type of instruction. Because the interest behind that decision — in strictly separating church and state — is an important one, and because education in religious schools is still allowed, there is no unconstitutional discrimination against religion and no violation of the Free Exercise or Establishment clauses.

9.15.   **Answer (B) is correct.** In *Epperson v. Arkansas*, 393 U.S. 97 (1968), the Court held that Arkansas' anti-evolution statute was unconstitutional. The Court concluded that the state prohibited the teaching of evolution in order to further a particular religious belief, and therefore that the state had impermissibly favored religion. Answer (B) is correct because it reflects the holding in *Epperson*.

Answer (A) is incorrect because it suggests that state officials have control of their curriculum (which is true), but it fails to take into account the Establishment Clause-based limitations on such control.

Answer (C) is incorrect because *Epperson* did not hold that anti-evolution statutes are permissible provided that the state does not mandate the teaching of creationism.

Answer (D) is incorrect because *Epperson* did not address whether the teaching of evolution is equivalent to "secular humanism."

9.16.   **Answer (D) is correct.** The *Lemon* test requires that, in order to survive

Establishment Clause scrutiny, government action (1) have a secular purpose, (2) not have the primary effect of inhibiting or advancing religion, and (3) not entangle government in religious matters. The second prong of this test reflects an approach to the First Amendment where promotion of religion generally, as opposed to non-religion, is constitutionally suspect. Answer (D) is correct because it correctly identifies the third prong of the *Lemon* test, concern with government entanglement with religion, while also noting that that issue is not the only *Lemon* requirement.

Answer (A) is incorrect because *Lemon* did not hold that the Establishment Clause allows government to promote religion in general as long as it does not single out any particular religion for especially favorable or unfavorable treatment. *Lemon* is generally understood as an opinion that adopts a "separationist" approach to the Establishment Clause, rather than a "non-preferentialist" approach that allows government to prefer religion in general as long as it does not favor one particular religion over another.

Answer (B) is incorrect because *Lemon* held open the possibility that a government action could violate the Establishment Clause even if it was motivated by a secular intent. For example, a statute with a secular intent could still entangle government with religion to an unacceptable extent.

Answer (C) is incorrect because *Lemon* looks both to intent (in the first prong) and effects (in the second).

9.17.   **Answer (C) is correct** because a program like New Kent's would entangle the government with religion and thus violate *Lemon. See* ERWIN CHEMERINSKY, CONSTITUTIONAL LAW: PRINCIPLES AND POLICIES 1162 (2d ed. 2002).

Answer (A) is incorrect because it provides that program will be upheld if the government is performing the monitoring "very closely." As Answer (C) suggests, such close monitoring creates an excessive entanglement with religion thereby rendering the program invalid.

Answer (B) is incorrect because monitoring of this sort, under either this formula or the one in answer (A), would involve government entanglement with religion and thus violate the rule of *Lemon v. Kurtzman*, 403 U.S. 602 (1971), which requires, in part, that government action not entangle the government with religion.

Answer (D) is incorrect because sometimes state aid to parochial schools is constitutional. *See, e.g., Mitchell v. Helms*, 530 U.S. 793 (2000).

9.18.   **Answer (C) is correct** because it reflects the result in *Good News Club v. Milford*, 533 U.S. 98 (2001). In that case, which had analogous facts to this hypothetical, the Court held that the school did not have a valid Establishment Clause-based interest in preventing a Bible study group from meeting on campus when other community groups were able to use the school's meeting facilities. On the contrary, allowing the club to meet would simply accommodate the club's religious beliefs in a content-neutral manner.

Answer (A) is incorrect because *Good News Club* did not find an Establishment

Clause violation.

Answer (B) is incorrect because *Good News Club* did not hold that the school has a point that it would be violating the Establishment Clause if it allowed the group to meet in the high school.

Answer (D) is incorrect because the type of monitoring implicit in the answer would clash with *Lemon v. Kurtzman*, 403 U.S. 602 (1971), where the Court held that the Establishment Clause is violated if, among other things, the government action entangles the government with religion. Here, the monitoring would force the government to make judgments about religious instruction which would amount to this sort of entanglement.

9.19.   **Answer (B) is correct** because it reflects the result and analysis in *Tilton v. Richardson*, 403 U.S. 672 (1971). Following the test in *Lemon v. Kurtzman*, 403 U.S. 602 (1971), which required, among other things, that government action have a legitimate secular purpose, the Court in *Tilton* noted that the purpose of the aid was secular — to promote expanded educational opportunities.

Answer (A) is incorrect because *Tilton* made clear that even direct aid to religious schools would be upheld under certain circumstances.

Answer (C) is incorrect because sometimes aid to religious institutions is unconstitutional. *E.g., Committee v. Public Education v. Nyquist*, 413 U.S. 756 (1973) (striking down government aid to religious schools).

Answer (D) is incorrect because such indirect effects are not addressed by *Lemon*, which asks, among other things, whether the *primary* effect of the government action was the promotion or inhibition of religion. Moreover, *Tilton* itself refutes this rationale, since the aid in that case presumably made religious education cheaper by defraying the cost of the secular component of the school's educational program.

9.20.   **Answer (C) is correct** because it states the result and reasoning from *Cutter v. Wilkinson*, 544 U.S. 709 (2005), where the Court rejected a facial challenge to the Religious Land Use and Institutionalized Persons Act (RLUIPA), which is in relevant part the statute assumed in this question.

Answer (A) is incorrect because in *Cutter*, the Court explicitly rejected the reasoning reflected in Answer (A).

Answer (B) is incorrect because the Establishment Clause does apply to the states; it is simply not violated by this statute.

Answer (D) is incorrect because the Court in *Cutter* made clear that other, longstanding protections for free exercise rights, such as a state's provision of chaplains to prison inmates, does not violate the Establishment Clause.

9.21.   **Answer (D) is correct** because all three of the theories reflected in answers (A), (B), and (C) have been adopted by the Supreme Court at one time or another, but none has become the definitive approach. *See* ERWIN CHEMERINSKY, CONSTITUTIONAL LAW: PRINCIPLES AND POLICIES 1149–1155 (2d ed. 2002).

Answer (A) is incorrect because the Supreme Court has not consistently approached Establishment Clause cases from a strict separationist perspective that is inherently skeptical of all government aid to religion. *Id.*

Answer (B) is incorrect because the Supreme Court has not consistently approached Establishment Clause cases from a perspective that seeks to accommodate government encouragement of religion generally, as long as it does not prefer one religion over another. *Id.*

Answer (C) is incorrect because the Supreme Court has not consistently approached Establishment Clause cases from a perspective that seeks to ensure government neutrality as between religion and non-religion. *Id.*

9.22.   **Answer (C) is correct** because it most closely states the rule from *McCreary County v. ACLU*, 545 U.S. 844 (2005), which features closely analogous facts.

Answer (A) is incorrect because the Establishment Clause is generally understood to prohibit more than simply state action that coerces profession of a particular religious belief.

Answer (B) is incorrect because in *McCreary County*, the Court reaffirmed the requirement that government must have a legitimate secular purpose behind every action, and concluded that the county's earlier postings were relevant to determining the intent of the final decision to post the larger set of documents. Here, the commissioners secularized the display only in response to the litigation, suggesting that they did not have a legitimate secular objective.

Answer (D) is incorrect because it goes too far; it has never been the case that government was prohibited from displaying any information with a potentially religious message, such as a religious painting displayed in a museum.

9.23.   **Answer (C) is correct** (as the least relevant inquiry) because this was not a weighty inquiry in *Van Orden v. Perry*, 545 U.S. 677 (2005), the case whose facts are most closely analogous to those in this question. The factor in Answer (C) is too broad, given that the Court has never questioned the constitutionality of, for example, government placing religious paintings in museums or a depiction Moses on the interior frieze of the Supreme Court's courtroom. Thus, (C) is least likely to be influential in resolving this case, and is therefore the correct answer.

Answer (A) is incorrect because the plurality in *Van Orden* concluded that monuments of this sort, which spoke to a state's historical heritage, were generally constitutional; thus, the fact in Answer (A) is relevant (and hence, the wrong answer here).

Answer (B) is incorrect because the length of the monument's existence on the capitol grounds without controversy was relevant to Justice Breyer's analysis in *Van Orden*, and he provided the fifth vote for upholding the Texas display in that case. Thus, this factor would also be potentially quite relevant and hence the incorrect answer here.

Answer (D) is incorrect for a similar reason as the one given for Answer (A); the plurality in *Van Orden* relied in part on this factor in upholding the Ten

Commandments display in that case.

10.1. **Answer (D) is correct** because it is the inaccurate statement. Although many immigrants came to the Americas in an effort to escape religious persecution, it is not clear that they were interested in creating a place of tolerance for all religions and all sects. On the contrary, some religious groups who immigrated to the American colonies sought to discriminate against those who did not agree with them. See generally the discussion in the majority opinion in *Everson v. Bd. of Education*, 330 U.S. 1 (1947).

Answer (A) is incorrect because it is an accurate statement. Many early immigrants to the American colonies came fleeing religious persecution in Europe. *See Everson, supra.*

Answer (B) is incorrect because it is an accurate statement. A significant percentage of immigrants to the American colonies came seeking to escape being taxed to support religions to which they did not belong. *See Everson, supra.*

Answer (C) is incorrect because it is an accurate statement. A significant percentage of immigrants to the American colonies came seeking a place where they could freely exercise their religious beliefs. *See Everson, supra.*

10.2. **Answer (C) is the correct answer.** There have been instances when the Free Exercise Clause has been used to trump the obligations of a statute through an accommodation to a religious practice. *See, e.g., Wisconsin v. Yoder*, 406 U.S. 205 (1972) (allowing Amish parents to violate a mandatory school attendance rule for religious reasons).

Answer (A) is incorrect. It is not correct to state that, in every instance when there is a conflict between the obligations of a law and an individual's religious beliefs, the Free Exercise Clause requires require that the obligations of state law give way to the religious practice. *See, e.g., Employment Div. v. Smith*, 494 U.S. 872 (1990) (generally applicable laws normally do not violate the Free Exercise Clause even if they compel conduct in conflict with religious beliefs).

Answer (B) is incorrect. It is not correct to state that, in the history of the Free Exercise Clause, the obligations of a statute have never been forced to give way to a religious concern or practice. *See, e.g., Yoder.*

Answer (D) is incorrect. The Establishment Clause does not always prohibit the states from accommodating a religious belief when there is a conflict with the obligations of a state law. *See, e.g., Yoder.*

10.3. **Answer (D) is correct** because answers (A), (B), and (C) are all inaccurate statements of the law. However, the Court has encountered great difficulty in defining religion. *See* ERWIN CHEMERINSKY, CONSTITUTIONAL LAW: PRINCIPLES AND POLICIES 1144 (2d ed. 2002).

Answer (A) is incorrect because the Court has held that an individual's belief may deviate from the official dogma of the religion he purports to espouse. *See Thomas v. Review Board*, 450 U.S. 707 (1981).

Answer (B) is incorrect because the Supreme Court has indicated that it may be appropriate for courts to inquire into the sincerity of the individual's belief. *See* ERWIN CHEMERINSKY, CONSTITUTIONAL LAW: PRINCIPLES AND POLICIES 1147 (2d ed. 2002).

Answer (C) is incorrect because the Supreme Court has rejected the idea that there are two definitions of religion, one for purposes of the Establishment Clause and one for purposes of the Free Exercise Clause. *See Everson v. Board of Education*, 330 U.S. 1 (1947).

10.4. In *Everson v. Board of Education*, 330 U.S. 1 (1947), the Court gave a lengthy explanation of those reasons:

> A large proportion of the early settlers of this country came here from Europe to escape the bondage of laws which compelled them to support and attend government favored churches. . . . Catholics had persecuted Protestants, Protestants had persecuted Catholics, Protestant sects had persecuted other Protestant sects, Catholics of one shade of belief had persecuted Catholics of another shade of belief, and all of these had from time to time persecuted Jews. In efforts to force loyalty to whatever religious group happened to be on top and in league with the government of a particular time and place, men and women had been fined, cast in jail, cruelly tortured, and killed. Among the offenses for which these punishments had been inflicted were such things as speaking disrespectfully of the views of ministers of government-established churches, nonattendance at those churches, expressions of non-belief in their doctrines, and failure to pay taxes and tithes to support them.
>
> These practices of the old world were transplanted to [and] thrived in the soil of the new America. The very charters granted by the English Crown [authorized] individuals and companies to erect religious establishments which all, whether believers or non-believers, would be required to support and attend. [E]xercise of this authority was accompanied by a repetition of many of the old world practices and persecutions. Catholics found themselves hounded and proscribed because of their faith; Quakers who followed their conscience went to jail; Baptists were peculiarly obnoxious to certain dominant Protestant sects; men and women of varied faiths who happened to be in a minority in a particular locality were persecuted because they steadfastly persisted in worshipping God only as their own consciences dictated. And all of these dissenters were compelled to pay tithes and taxes to support government-sponsored churches whose ministers preached inflammatory sermons designed to strengthen and consolidate the established faith by generating a burning hatred against dissenters.

These practices became so commonplace as to shock the freedom-loving colonials into a feeling of abhorrence. The imposition of taxes to pay ministers' salaries and to build and maintain churches and church property aroused their indignation. It was these feelings which found expression in the First Amendment. [Virginia] provided a great stimulus. . . . The people there, as elsewhere, reached the conviction that individual religious liberty could be achieved best under a government which was stripped of all power to tax, to support, or otherwise to assist any or all religions, or to interfere with the beliefs of any religious individual or group.

The movement toward this end reached its dramatic climax in Virginia in 1785–86 when the Virginia legislative body was about to renew Virginia's tax levy for the support of the established church. Thomas Jefferson and James Madison led the fight against this tax. Madison wrote his great Memorial and Remonstrance against the law. In it, he eloquently argued that a true religion did not need the support of law; that no person, either believer or non-believer, should be taxed to support a religious institution of any kind; that the best interest of a society required that the minds of men always be wholly free; and that cruel persecutions were the inevitable result of government-established religions. Madison's Remonstrance received strong support throughout Virginia, and the Assembly postponed consideration of the proposed tax measure until its next session. When the proposal came up for consideration at that session, it not only died in committee, but the Assembly enacted the famous "Virginia Bill for Religious Liberty" originally written by Thomas Jefferson. . . .

[T]he provisions of the First Amendment [had] the same objective and were intended to provide the same protection against governmental intrusion on religious liberty as the Virginia statute. . . .

10.5. **Answer (D) is correct** because *United States v. Ballard*, 322 U.S. 78 (1944), did not hold that Ballard could be convicted of fraud because he knowingly made false statements about religious matters. Such a conviction, the Court stated, would amount to a conviction for heresy.

Answer (A) is incorrect because *Ballard* stated that freedom of religious belief "embraces the right to maintain theories of life and of death and of the hereafter which are rank heresy to followers of the orthodox faiths."

Answer (B) is incorrect because *Ballard* stated that freedom of thought, which includes freedom of religious belief, is basic in a society of free men.

Answer (C) is incorrect because *Ballard* stated that courts may not inquire into the truth or falsity of a person's religious beliefs.

10.6. In *Wisconsin v. Yoder*, 406 U.S. 205 (1972), the Court accepted the Old Order Amish's argument about their way of life. In other words, that way of life was so connected to the Old Order Amish's religious practices that it was entitled to constitutional protection: "[The record] abundantly supports the claim that the traditional way of life of the Amish is not merely a matter of personal preference, but one of deep religious conviction, shared by an organized group, and intimately related to daily living. . . .'"

10.7. **Answer (C) is correct.** In *Thomas v. Review Board*, 450 U.S. 707 (1981), the Court explicitly stated that "[i]t is not within the judicial function and judicial competence to inquire whether the petitioner or his fellow worker [of the same religion] more correctly perceived the commands of their common faith. Courts are not arbiters of scriptural interpretation." As a result, Answer (C) is correct.

Answer (A) is incorrect because the Court stated that "the guarantee of free exercise is not limited to beliefs which are shared by all of the members of a religious sect."

Answer (B) is incorrect because the Court did not require that the claimant be able to articulate his religious views "with the clarity and precision that a more sophisticated person might employ."

Answer (D) is incorrect because the Court did not hold that courts have an obligation to inquire into the accuracy of a person's interpretation of his religion's beliefs. Indeed, the Court viewed such an inquiry as beyond the competence of courts.

10.8. **Answer (B) is correct** because in *Reynolds*, the Court distinguished between "belief" and "conduct," and concluded that the government had broad authority to prohibit religiously-motivated conduct, such as polygamy in this case.

Answer (A) is incorrect because the Court did not hold that the practice of polygamy was protected under the Free Exercise Clause.

Answer (C) is incorrect since the Court did not rule on whether polygamy is an essential aspect of Mormonism. Indeed, courts generally do not decide on the centrality of any particular aspect of a religion, as doing so would be an inappropriate government intrusion into that religion.

Answer (D) is incorrect because the Court allowed the government to ban polygamy even though it was largely engaged in for religious reasons.

10.9. **Answer (A) is correct** because in *Sherbert*, the Court held that a "[g]overnmental imposition of such a choice [as that required by the state unemployment law] puts the same kind of burden upon the free exercise of religion as would a fine imposed against [the claimant] for her Saturday worship."

Answer (B) is incorrect because *Sherbert* did not hold that the Free Exercise Clause is inapplicable to "peripheral" religious beliefs like the claimant's refusal to work on Saturday. Courts generally do not decide whether a particular religious practice is central or peripheral to a plaintiff's religion, given the government intrusion on religious matters such an inquiry would impose.

Answer (C) is incorrect because *Sherbert* did not hold that the claimant's refusal to work constituted "conduct" and therefore fell outside the protection of the Free Exercise Clause.

Answer (D) is incorrect because *Sherbert* did not hold that the Free Exercise Clause allows a state to deny unemployment compensation when a person refuses offered work for religious reasons. Indeed, the Court ruled in favor of the claimant.

10.10. Such a constitutional provision would be struck down under the Establishment Clause. In *Torcaso v. Watkins*, 367 U.S. 488 (1961), a state constitution required declaration of a belief in God as a prerequisite to assuming public office. The Court struck the law down, holding that the government may not compel anyone to affirm or deny a religious belief. It stated, quoting its Establishment Clause analysis in *Everson v. Bd. of Education*, 330 U.S. 1 (1947): "The 'establishment of religion' clause of the First Amendment means at least this: Neither a state nor the Federal Government can set up a church. Neither can pass laws which aid one religion, aid all religions, or prefer one religion over another. Neither can force nor influence a person to go to or to remain away from church against his will or force him to profess a belief or disbelief in any religion."

10.11. **Answer (C) is correct.** In *Smith*, the Court held that respondents were not protected because the Court has never held that an individual's religious beliefs excuse him from compliance with an otherwise valid law of general applicability prohibiting conduct that the State is free to regulate. The Court distinguished cases such as *Wisconsin v. Yoder*, 406 U.S. 205 (1972) (allowing the Amish to violate a compulsory school attendance law) on the ground that cases such as *Yoder* involved both the combination of a Free Exercise claim *and* another constitutional rights claim (for example, in *Yoder*, the due process right to direct the upbringing of one's children). It further distinguished cases like *Sherbert v. Verner*, 374 U.S. 398 (1963), on the ground that unemployment compensation claims were structurally set up to allow individualized consideration of claimant's religious exercise-based reasons for not accepting particular work. Since the drug law was a valid rule of general applicability there was no right to unemployment compensation when it was denied because of the employee had committed misconduct.

Answer (A) is incorrect because *Smith* ruled against the employees who made this claim.

Answer (B) is incorrect because in *Smith* the Court did not demand that the law be supported by a compelling government interest. This was the position taken by the dissent and Justice O'Connor's concurrence in the judgment, not the majority.

Answer (D) is incorrect because the Court did not protect the employees' religiously-motivated use of peyote.

10.12. **Answer (B) is correct.** In *Church of the Lukumi*, the Court held that the law violates the Free Exercise Clause if it discriminates against some or all religious beliefs or regulates or prohibits conduct because it is undertaken for religious reasons.

Answer (A) is incorrect because the Court did not rely on the belief-conduct distinction; indeed, it protected the conduct at issue here.

Answer (C) is incorrect because, contrary to this answer, the Court held that the Santeria's practice was constitutionally protected.

Answer (D) is incorrect because the Court recognized that the law's exceptions essentially meant that the law targeted religious practice.

10.13. **Answer (B) is correct** because in *Lyng*, the Court stated that government "simply could not operate if it were required to satisfy every citizen's religious needs and desires. A broad range of government activities — from social welfare programs to foreign aid to conservation projects — will always be considered essential to the spiritual well-being of some citizens, often on the basis of sincerely held religious beliefs."

Answer (A) is incorrect because the Court allowed the USFS to build the road.

Answer (C) is incorrect because the Court refused to enmesh itself in questions about whether the Indians' beliefs were "central" to their religion.

Answer (D) is incorrect because the Court did not hold that the Free Exercise Clause absolutely protects Indian burial grounds. Indeed, it ruled against the religion claim in this case.

10.14. **Answer (C) is correct** because *Kiryas Joel* held that the district was unconstitutional.

Answer (A) is incorrect because the Court held that the special treatment provided the religious group in this case crossed the line from accommodation to singling out a sect for special favorable treatment.

Answer (B) is incorrect because the Court held that granting special treatment to a particular religion violates the Establishment Clause.

Answer (D) is incorrect because the Court did not hold that the Establishment Clause does not apply to the creation of special school districts. The Establishment Clause applies to any government action, such as, here, the creation of a school district.

10.15. **Answer (B) is correct**. In *Rosenberger*, the Court held that the denial constituted an unconstitutional viewpoint-based speech discrimination.

Answer (A) is incorrect because the Court concluded that funding the speech would not have violated the Establishment Clause.

Answer (C) is incorrect because the Court concluded that funding the speech would not have violated the Establishment Clause.

Answer (D) is incorrect because the *Rosenberger* Court in fact considered whether funding the religious speech would violate the Establishment Clause.

10.16. In *United States v. Lee*, 455 U.S. 252 (1982), the Court held that a member of the Old Order Amish was not entitled to an exemption from this tax:

> Because the social security system is nationwide, the governmental interest is apparent. The social security system [serves] the public interest

by providing a comprehensive insurance system with a variety of benefits available to all participants, with costs shared by employers and employees. [M]andatory participation is indispensable to the fiscal vitality of the social security system. [Unlike] the situation presented in *Wisconsin v. Yoder*, 406 U.S. 205 (1972) [(upholding Amish refusal to comply with mandatory school attendance laws)], it would be difficult to accommodate the comprehensive social security system with myriad exceptions flowing from a wide variety of religious beliefs. . . .

10.17. **Answer (B) is correct** because, in *Jimmy Swaggart* the Court upheld the tax as applied to religious literature because it was a neutral tax applicable to all goods and services.

Answer (A) is incorrect because it suggests that the Court struck the tax down, which it did not.

Answer (C) is incorrect because it suggests that state and local governments have an "absolute right" to tax, which is too strong a statement.

Answer (D) is incorrect because the Court did not hold that religious groups cannot object to taxation.

10.18. There is little doubt that the state interest in highway safety is a compelling interest. The question is whether there are "reasonable alternatives" that justify an exemption from the state regulation. In this case, the Amish have demonstrated a burden on their religious beliefs (displaying the triangle violates their religious belief against displaying "loud colors" and "worldly symbols"), and have offered to line the outside of their buggies with silver reflective tape and to adorn the buggies with lighted red lanterns. The state deems these actions insufficient. Courts usually resolve this issue in favor of the states. *See State v. Hershberger*, 462 N.W.2d 393 (Minn. 1990). This would especially be the case after *Employment Division v. Smith*, 494 U.S. 872 (1990), where the Supreme Court held that neutral laws of general applicability will usually be applied to religiously-motivated conduct (or, here, failure to act), even if it has the effect of burdening religion.

10.19. **Answer (B) is correct** because in *Cantwell*, the Court held that the permit requirement violated the Cantwells' right to freely exercise their religion, in part because of the discretion the government official had to determine whether the desired speech was in fact on behalf of a religion.

Answer (A) is incorrect because in *Cantwell*, the Court did not limit the right to free exercise simply to the right to attend religious services of one's choice.

Answer (C) is incorrect because in *Cantwell*, the Court relied in part on the Free Exercise Clause to strike down the government action.

Answer (D) is incorrect because in *Cantwell*, the Court did not hold that the Establishment Clause precludes the government from regulating the distribution of religious literature. Reasonable time, place, and manner restrictions on such conduct may be upheld.

10.20. **Answer (A) is correct** because in *Goldman*, the Court upheld the prohibition on the basis that the military is by definition a specialized society separate from civilian society, and that the interests of military members can be subordinated to the interests and desires of the individual to the needs of the service.

Answer (B) is incorrect because *Goldman* did not uphold the soldier's Free Exercise claim.

Answer (C) is incorrect because *Goldman* did not hold that the regulation violated the Establishment Clause.

Answer (D) is incorrect because *Goldman* did not hold that the Free Exercise Clause protects all religious symbols. Indeed, *Goldman* rejected the plaintiff's claim that the clause protected his right to wear a yarmulke.

10.21. **Answer (C) is correct.** In *O'Lone*, the Court upheld the prison regulation on the ground that:

> "[C]onvicted prisoners do not forfeit all constitutional protections by reason of their conviction and confinement in prison." However, "[l]awful incarceration brings about the necessary withdrawal or limitation of many privileges and rights, a retraction justified by the considerations underlying our penal system." [E]valuation of penological objectives is committed to the considered judgment of prison administrators. . . . [P]rison officials have acted in a reasonable manner. [Prison] officials testified that the returns from outside work details generated congestion and delays at the main gate, a high risk area in any event. Return requests also placed pressure on guards supervising outside details, who previously were required to evaluate each reason possibly justifying a return to the facilities and either accept or reject that reason. Rehabilitative concerns further supported the policy. . . ."

Answer (A) is incorrect because it suggests that the prison regulation was invalid; moreover, courts have never held that prisoners have absolute rights to free exercise.

Answer (B) is incorrect because the Court did not subject the regulations to this level of searching scrutiny.

Answer (D) is incorrect because the Court did not hold that the Free Exercise Clause is inapplicable in the prison context.

FINAL EXAM ANSWERS

1. **Answer (C) is correct** because *New York Times*, which imposed the actual malice requirement, involved a commentary on the actions of a public official.

   Answer (A) is incorrect because *Sullivan* did not hold that the actual malice standard should be applied only to political speech. Instead, it applied that standard to all comment on many types of actions by public officials.

   Answer (B) is incorrect because *Sullivan* applied the actual malice standard to a political advertisement.

   Answer (D) is incorrect because *Sullivan* did not hold that the actual malice standard should apply to speech relating to private figures.

2. In *Curtis Publishing Co. v. Butts*, 388 U.S. 130 (1967), the Court first referred to the concept of a "vortex" public figure. In some instances, individuals have such fame that they are regarded as public figures for all purposes and all situations. In other instances, individuals may not be famous, but have become so by entering an important public controversy. In a companion case decided with *Curtis Publishing*, the Court held that an individual became a public figure "by his purposeful activity amounting to a thrusting of his personality into the 'vortex' of an important public controversy."

3. **Answer (B) is correct** because *Hustler Magazine* held that even outrageous parodies are entitled to constitutional protection.

   Answer (A) is incorrect because *Hustler Magazine* did not hold that outrageous parodies are entitled to constitutional protection.

   Answer (C) is incorrect because *Hustler Magazine* did not hold that parodies must be "fair" to be accorded constitutional protection.

   Answer (D) is incorrect because *Hustler Magazine* did not hold that parodies have nothing to do with free speech.

4. **Answer (C) is correct** because it corresponds to the *Miller v. California*, 413 U.S. 15 (1973), standard of what constitutes obscenity. The book can possibly be banned because the descriptions of Denver probably do not rise to the level of "serious literary, artistic, political, or scientific value" that the Supreme Court held in *Miller* makes a work non-obscene and thus constitutionally protected. Before that becomes a definite conclusion, however, the other *Miller* requirements have to be analyzed.

   Answer (A) is incorrect because *Miller* did not hold that any speech dealing with sexual expression is protected just like speech dealing with any other type of activity. Rather, *Miller* allowed government to ban the sale or distribution of obscene speech.

   Answer (B) is incorrect because the modern standard for obscenity, from *Miller*, requires, among other things, that the work lack "serious literary, artistic, political, or scientific value" before it can be held to be banned. Answer (B's) standard is too lenient for it to be a correct answer.

Answer (D) is incorrect because, while appeal to the prurient interest is a factor in the *Miller* test, it is not the only factor, and satisfaction of that factor by itself does not justify suppression of the speech.

5.   **Answer (B) is correct,** because it reflects the Supreme Court's decision in *Ashcroft v. Free Speech Coalition*, 535 U.S. 234 (2002). In that case, the Court noted that the main harm of child pornography lies in its exploitation of children; because virtual child pornography is at least potentially free of that harm, the Court protected it.

Answer (A) is incorrect because *Ashcroft* did not hold that the difficulty of determining whether virtual child pornography actually used live models justified a prohibition on its possession.

Answer (C) is incorrect because *Ashcroft* did not hold that the harm of child pornography lies in the appetites it feeds for abusing children, but rather, in the harms to the actual child models.

Answer (D) is incorrect. The harm in child pornography lies not in its obscenity *per se*, but rather in the harm its production causes to the child models. Thus, the *Miller* obscenity test is irrelevant to the constitutional status of child pornography.

6.   **Answer (C) is correct**. The state's power to regulate alcohol transactions, either under the 21st Amendment or its general police power, does not mean that it can simply take the "lesser" step of restricting speech about that transaction. *44 Liquormart v. Rhode Island*, 517 U.S. 484 (1996). Answer (C) is correct because *44 Liquormart* struck down an analogous speech restriction on alcohol, concluding that the state had other ways to accomplish its legitimate goals, short of regulating speech.

Answer (A) is incorrect because it is not correct to state that the 21st Amendment absolves the states of the need to satisfy First Amendment standards when regulating alcohol advertising. *44 Liquormart.*

Answer (B) is incorrect because the Court has rejected this sort of greater-includes-the-lesser analysis of commercial speech regulation. *44 Liquormart.*

Answer (D) is incorrect because commercial speech ostensibly still gets the intermediate level of scrutiny announced in *Central Hudson Gas v. Public Service Comm'n*, 447 U.S. 557 (1980), not strict scrutiny.

7.   **Answer (C) is correct** because it states the rule from *West Virginia St. Bd. of Educ. v. Barnette*, 319 U.S. 624 (1943). In that case the Court held that government could not force people to have or enunciate a particular opinion, as this clashed with the right of free thought implicit in the First Amendment.

Answer (A) is incorrect because even though government might have an interest in fostering patriotism, under *Barnette* it could not promote that interest by forcing people to speak.

Answer (B) is incorrect because under *Barnette*, being forced to speak is as serious a First Amendment violation as being prevented from speaking.

Answer (D) is incorrect because government does have a legitimate interest in fostering certain viewpoints, *Rust v. Sullivan*, 500 U.S. 173 (1991) (upholding a prohibition on abortion counseling in a government-funded health program); it just can't do so in a way that violates the right to speak.

8. Mandy's defense to the incitement charge would be judged under the standards of *Bradenburg v. Ohio*, 395 U.S. 444 (1969). Under *Brandenburg*, speech can be punished as incitement to illegal action only if (1) the speaker intended to incite immediate unlawful conduct and (2) it was likely that the speaker would in fact succeed. Here, the rhetorical nature of her speech, plus the lack of any direct encouragement to the crowd to commit the illegal act, probably means that the first prong of the test has not been satisfied. Thus, the incitement charge cannot stand.

9. Mandy's defense to the second charge raises a question of symbolic speech. Conduct that has communicative content can nevertheless can be punished by government if: (1) the regulation is otherwise within the constitutional power of the government; (2) regulation of the action is not motivated by a desire to penalize expression; (3) the government has an important interest in preventing the non-speech related harms that flow from the conduct; and (4) the incidental restriction on expression is no greater than that essential to the furtherance of that interest. Here, the identification of voters is clearly within the constitutional power of the local government, which runs local elections. Also, the government has a legitimate interest in being able to identify voters, and there is no evidence that the government was motivated by a desire to penalize Mandy's expression. Finally, there is probably no less speech-restrictive way of ensuring voter identification. Thus, it is likely that this charge can stand consistent with the First Amendment.

10. **Answer (B) is correct.** In *Cohen v. California*, 403 U.S. 15 (1971), the Supreme Court articulated a context-specific test for determining when speech reached the level of unprotected "fighting words." Under that test, a court would have to examine the context of the incident to determine whether there was a likelihood that someone would respond to Renfro's speech with violence, for example, if the speech was directed to someone as a direct taunt. Answer (B) is correct because, if established, it suggests that Renfro was directing his expression toward a particular person. This may not be strong support for a conviction, but it is stronger than the support provided by the other answer choices.

Answer (A) is incorrect because it provides only weak support for this requirement, since it does not indicate that any of the spectators thought anything bad about Renfro's actions.

Answer (C) is incorrect because the context-specific analysis required by *Cohen* requires more than determining what, in the abstract, a reasonable person would think of the speech.

Answer (D) is incorrect. Because Answer (B) is better than (A) and (C), Answer (D) is necessarily incorrect.

11. **Answer (B) is correct** because under *Ferber v. New York*, 458 U.S. 747 (1982),

pornography that contains pictures of actual child models is unprotected under the First Amendment due to the harm it causes the child models.

Answer (A) is incorrect because child pornography that is non-obscene under *Miller* is still unprotected if it uses child models.

Answer (C) is incorrect because *Ferber*'s concern for the well-being of children means that even private possession of such material is not protected, unlike, for example, in *Stanley v. Georgia*, 394 U.S. 557 (1969), where the pornography was not child pornography. *Osborne v. Ohio*, 495 U.S. 103 (1990).

Answer (D) is incorrect because it is too broad; under *Miller v. California*, 413 U.S. 15 (1973), some pornographic material is not obscene, and thus enjoys at least some constitutional protection if it does not use child models.

12. Probably not. The ordinance clearly restricts commercial speech. Under the test set forth in *Central Hudson Gas v. Public Service Comm'n*, 447 U.S. 557 (1980), commercial speech can be regulated only if the government has a substantial interest, which the regulation directly advances, and a more limited restriction on speech would not serve that interest. Moreover, for commercial speech to enjoy this kind of protection it must relate to a lawful activity and not be misleading. Here, the handbill speech clearly gets the protection of the commercial speech doctrine. Because the restriction is based on content, and because commercial speech gets some protection, the ordinance would probably be reviewed with some care. Most notably, a court would probably question why the restriction was only on commercial speech, and not on newspapers as well, when there is no evidence that handbills are the only or even main contributor to blight and litter. On that basis the court would probably strike the ordinance down.

13. **Answer (B) is correct** because, in *Tinker v. Des Moines Sch. Dist.*, 393 U.S. 503 (1969), the Court noted that students do not shed all their constitutional rights when they enter the school campus. However, *Tinker* also stated that the possibility of substantial disruption of educational activities might justify infringement of student expression. Answer (B) reflects the analysis in *Tinker*, and thus is the correct answer.

Answer (A) is incorrect since *Tinker* suggests that schools do not have near-complete control over the conduct of students while on campus.

Answer (C) is incorrect since the Court in *Tinker* recognized that the wearing of armbands is a form of expression entitled to First Amendment protection.

Answer (D) is incorrect since courts in cases such as *Ginsberg v. New York*, 393 U.S. 503 (1968), have recognized that the immaturity of children gives government extra reason to regulate their speech rights.

14. **Answer (A) is correct.** In *Reno v. ACLU*, 521 U.S. 844 (1997), the Supreme Court struck down a statute that contained a similar provision. The Court expressed concern that non-commercial operators, such as individuals posting information on websites or in chat rooms, would be subject to liability, and that the credit card access safe harbor in the statute was insufficient because many non-commercial

entities would find that requirement too hard to meet. This analysis suggests that answer (A) is correct.

Answer (B) is incorrect because, after *ACLU*, the protection of children, while still important, is not enough automatically to uphold a statute.

Answer (C) is incorrect because speech on the Internet does not enjoy absolute protection; like any other speech, it can be restricted if government satisfies the appropriate standard of First Amendment review.

Answer (D) is incorrect because, as long as the Internet is not a non-public government owned forum (which it is not, *see ACLU*), there is no reason to assume that more lenient speech restriction rules will apply.

15. **Answer (B) is correct.** In *Citizens United v. Federal Election Comm'n*, 130 S. Ct. 876 (2010), the Supreme Court held that identity-based distinctions with regard to who can speak on political issues are presumptively unconstitutional. It struck down a restriction on corporations of any sort using their general treasury funds to engage in political speech.

Answer (A) is incorrect because the *Citizens United* Court did not rely on this rationale for protecting speech by all corporations.

Answer (C) is incorrect after *Citizens United*. This was the correct answer prior to *Citizens United* because, in *Federal Election Comm'n v. Massachusetts Citizens for Life*, 479 U.S. 238 (1986), the Supreme Court distinguished between for-profit organizations and so-called "advocacy organizations," defined as corporations formed not to amass wealth but promote ideas. The Court there held that government had less leeway to restrict the rights of such advocacy organizations to spend money in support of those ideas. But *Citizens United* did away with this distinction.

Answer (D) is incorrect because even before *Citizens United* the relevant distinctions were not based on the motivations of the speaker.

16. **Answer (C) is correct** because in *Elrod v. Burns*, 427 U.S. 347 (1976), the Court struck down such patronage systems as unconstitutional violations of First Amendment rights of employees.

Answer (A) is incorrect because *Elrod* rejected the argument that the sheriff has significant latitude to make these personnel changes in light of the long history of political patronage in the United States. In *Elrod*, First Amendment guarantees trumped that interest.

Answer (B) is incorrect because *Elrod* rejected the argument that the sheriff has significant latitude to make these personnel changes based on party affiliation on the theory that subordinates of the same political persuasion will work more effectively together. The Court noted, among other things, that subordinates could always be dismissed for inefficient work.

Answer (D) is incorrect because *Elrod* recognized the importance of political affiliation to the First Amendment.

17.   **Answer (A) is correct** because, in *Greer v. Spock*, 424 U.S. 828 (1976), a case paralleling these facts, the Court held that a military base was a non-public forum, and that content-based restrictions on speech in that forum were permissible, as long as reasonable and viewpoint-neutral.

Answer (B) is incorrect because content-based restrictions on speech in public forums are constitutional as long as reasonable, *Greer*. Thus, there is no need for the military to be evenhanded as between religious, charity, or musical speech on the one hand and political speech on the other.

Answer (C) is incorrect because it goes even farther in the wrong direction than Answer (B), suggesting that even a content-neutral restriction would be constitutionally problematic. As indicated by *Greer*, that is not a correct statement of the law.

Answer (D) is incorrect because it goes too far in the other direction. If government imposes a *viewpoint*-based restriction on speech in a non-public forum, for example, allowing Democrats to speak on base but not Republicans, that restriction would probably be unconstitutional under standard First Amendment analysis, again as explained by *Greer*.

18.   **Answer (D) is correct**. The Court has never used the factor in Answer (D), and with good reason: almost by definition one could expect more speech if a particular property was called a public forum; that analysis, then, would cut in favor of any piece of government property being so labeled.

Answer (A) is incorrect because this factor has been cited by the Supreme Court as one of the factors in determining whether a piece of property is a public forum. *See* Erwin Chemerinsky, Constitutional Law: Principles and Policies 1102 (2d ed. 2002); *see also, e.g., Hague v. CIO*, 307 U.S. 496 (1939) (noting the fact that streets have historically used for speech).

Answer (B) is incorrect because this factor has been cited by the Supreme Court as one of the factors in determining whether a piece of property is a public forum. *See* Erwin Chemerinsky, Constitutional Law: Principles and Policies 1102 (2d ed. 2002); *see also, e.g., Adderly v. Florida*, 385 U.S. 39 (1996) (citing security concerns for deciding that a jail is not a public forum).

Answer (C) is incorrect because this factor has been cited by the Supreme Court as one of the factors in determining whether a piece of property is a public forum. *See* Erwin Chemerinsky, Constitutional Law: Principles and Policies 1102 (2d ed. 2002); *see also, e.g., International Society for Krishna Consciousness v. Lee*, 505 U.S. 672 (1992) (noting that airports' primary purpose is not for speech).

19.   **Answer (B) is correct** because it states the Supreme Court's explanation of sexual harassment speech in *R.A.V. v. St. Paul*, 505 U.S. 377 (1992). Even though *R.A.V.* did not directly deal with sexual harassment speech, the Court noted that sexual harassment laws are not a content-based restriction on speech since they are aimed at the substantive harm of gender discrimination, rather than at the content of the expression.

Answer (A) is incorrect because *R.A.V.* suggested that it rejects the notion that a rule against sexual harassment speech is a content-based restriction on speech since it prohibits sexual harassment but not other types of harassment (e.g., harassment based on sexual orientation). For that reason it would probably not subject such a rule to strict scrutiny.

Answer (C) is incorrect because, again under *R.A.V.*, the fact that harassment or fighting words is unprotected does not mean that content-based restrictions on that speech are acceptable; rather, more analysis is needed.

Answer (D) is incorrect because the Court in *R.A.V.* suggested that harassing speech is not protected by the Constitution.

20.   It probably would not. The facts here are very similar to those in *R.A.V. v. City of St. Paul*, 505 U.S. 377 (1992), where the Court struck down a similar ordinance. As in *R.A.V.*, the problem with the Quiet Haven ordinance is that it is content-based and that it is aimed at the primary expressive element of the speech — the message of hatred that causes the resentment, anger, etc. For that reason it will be subject to strict scrutiny, with the probable result that it will be struck down, since a content-neutral ban on cross-burning, or even a content-neutral ban on all hate speech, would take care of the problem while being less objectionable as a First Amendment matter. The fact that the Quiet Haven ordinance is explicitly limited to constitutionally unprotected "fighting words" does not help the town's case, since the objection to the ordinance is not that it punishes protected speech *per se*, but that it punishes unprotected speech in a content-based way.

21.   **Answer (C) is correct**. In *Freedman*, the Court held that the licensing scheme lacked sufficient procedural safeguards for confining the censor's action to judicially-determined constitutional limits, and therefore contains the same vice as a statute delegating excessive administrative discretion.

Answer (A) is incorrect because it is too broad; the Court in *Freedman* did not state such a broad rule. Indeed, the Court provided some guidelines for how a licensing scheme would be upheld as constitutional.

Answer (B) is incorrect because the Court did not hold that prior restraints on art and ideas are unconstitutional in all circumstances.

Answer (D) is incorrect because the Court did not hold that movies are not entitled to First Amendment protection. Indeed, in *Freedman* it protected movies under the First Amendment.

22.   **Answer (C) is correct** because, in cases like *Nebraska Press Association v. Stuart*, 427 U.S. 539 (1976), the Court has set forth a very strong presumption against gag orders as unconstitutional prior restraints on speech.

Answer (A) is incorrect because the press does have a First Amendment right to cover such events, even if on some occasions that right must give way to other rights.

Answer (B) is incorrect because this answer states the rule at too general a level;

the constitutionality of restrictions on press coverage of criminal trials turns on more precise analysis of the facts of each case against a given standard of review.

Answer (D) is incorrect because the Court has recognized that at times press coverage can impair the fairness of a trial. *See, e.g., Estes v. Texas*, 381 U.S. 532 (1965).

23. **Answer (D) is correct** because it is an inaccurate statement of what *Roberts* held. *Roberts* did not make such a broad statement; indeed, it rejected the Jaycees' right of association claim even though the group took positions on public issues.

Answer (A) is incorrect because *Roberts* did hold that the right of freedom of association extends to highly personal and intimate relationships.

Answer (B) is incorrect because *Roberts* did hold that a simple assertion by the discriminating organization is insufficient to uphold the right of association claim. *But see Boy Scouts of America v. Dale*, 530 U.S. 640 (2000) (potentially limiting this holding by deferring to the Scouts' own statements about what would interfere with their speech).

Answer (C) is incorrect because *Roberts* did hold that the membership selectivity of the organization is relevant to the analysis.

24. The statute would probably be upheld, as a similar Sunday-closing statute was in *McGowan v. Maryland*, 366 U.S. 420 (1961). Under *Lemon v. Kurtzman*, 403 U.S. 602 (1971), a statute alleged to violate the Establishment Clause is tested against three questions: (1) does it have a secular purpose; (2) does it have a primary effect that neither advances nor inhibits religion; and (3) does it foster an excessive government entanglement with religion? If the law either lacks a secular purpose, or has a primary effect of advancing or inhibiting religion, or fosters an excessive entanglement, it will be struck down. Here, the Lincoln statute clearly has the secular purpose of encouraging family life and it does not entangle government with religion. The only question is whether its primary effect is one that advances or inhibits religion. On these facts, and based on the Court's analysis in *McGowan*, a court would probably hold that the statute passes this test. Because Sundays have historically been the day of rest — even if that history was ultimately traceable to religious practice — and because it is probably the case that the primary effect of the law will be to promote family life (or at least the primary effect will not be religious), the court will probably find that this prong of *Lemon* is also satisfied, and that the statute is constitutional.

25. No (that is, the aid would be constitutional). In *Everson v. Bd. of Education*, 330 U.S. 1 (1947), the Supreme Court rejected an Establishment Clause challenge to such a plan, given that the assistance was provided without distinction to public and parochial students. Under *Lemon v. Kurtzman*, 403 U.S. 602 (1971), this plan would again probably survive. Under *Lemon*, a statute alleged to violate the Establishment Clause is tested against three questions: (1) does it have a secular purpose; (2) does it have a primary effect that neither advances nor inhibits religion; and (3) does it foster an excessive government entanglement with religion?

If the law either lacks a secular purpose, or has a primary effect of advancing or inhibiting religion, or fosters an excessive entanglement, it will be struck down. Here there is clearly a secular purpose — the safe transportation of young students and there is no entanglement between government and religion. Moreover, the primary effect is religion-neutral; the plan assists all students, regardless of where they attend school, and thus there is no concern that it will primarily assist religious education.

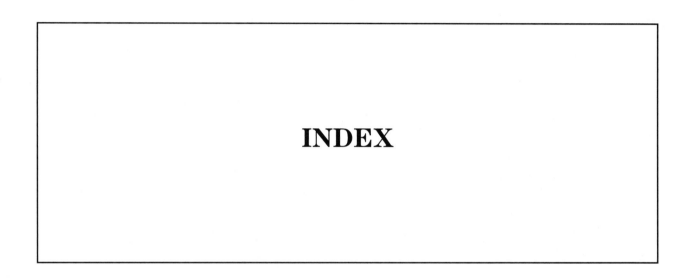

INDEX

INDEX